T0110630

FOR THE
FATHERLAND

FOR THE FATHERLAND

ILSA FANCHIN

iUniverse, Inc.
Bloomington

For the Fatherland

Copyright © 2013 by Ilsa Fanchin

All rights reserved. No part of this book may be used or reproduced by any means, graphic, electronic, or mechanical, including photocopying, recording, taping or by any information storage retrieval system without the written permission of the publisher except in the case of brief quotations embodied in critical articles and reviews.

iUniverse books may be ordered through booksellers or by contacting:

iUniverse
1663 Liberty Drive
Bloomington, IN 47403
www.iuniverse.com
1-800-Authors (1-800-288-4677)

Because of the dynamic nature of the Internet, any web addresses or links contained in this book may have changed since publication and may no longer be valid. The views expressed in this work are solely those of the author and do not necessarily reflect the views of the publisher, and the publisher hereby disclaims any responsibility for them.

Any people depicted in stock imagery provided by Thinkstock are models, and such images are being used for illustrative purposes only.
Certain stock imagery © Thinkstock.

ISBN: 978-1-4759-6338-0 (sc)
ISBN: 978-1-4759-6339-7 (ebk)

Printed in the United States of America

iUniverse rev. date: 1/10/2013

CONTENTS

To my son, Michael.
His persistence, knowledge, and great patience
gave me the courage to write this story.

ACKNOWLEDGMENT

To my fellow writers of Los Escribientes Writers Club for their editing and honest critiques.

PROLOGUE

In October 1944, in Frankfurt am Main, Germany, the fifth year of World War II escalated. Recorded are the last eight months of the war as seen through my eyes. The unconditional surrender of the German armed forces came on May 8, 1945.

In the middle of October, I received my draft notice, along with other young, *unmarried* twenty-two-year-old women who were physically able and would be employed in nonsensitive positions not vital for the war effort. Other age groups were to follow at a later date. We served on searchlights and replaced young male soldiers who had been called to combat on several fronts of fighting. Searchlights, always in close proximity of antiaircraft guns called FLAK (*Flug Abwehr Kanone*), were considered an effective defense against high-flying, bomb-carrying Allied planes.

Mixed among approximately three hundred young women draftees, I boarded a special train to the large industrial town of Leipzig, about 320 miles away in the eastern part of Germany. Our induction took place at a Leipzig military barracks. We underwent physicals and received uniforms and large metal brooches—badges of our loyalty to be worn at all times. A mandatory oath "to serve the Fatherland" followed in a solemn ritual.

Subsequently forty-nine draftees and the group leader were housed on the second floor of a former theater building in a small village near Leipzig. We trained in the correct use and maintenance of a searchlight at a nearby searchlight battery.

Under primitive conditions during a bitterly cold winter, we coped with our lot as best we could.

1

LIFE AT HOME

In my hometown, the large industrial city of Offenbach am Main, countless Allied bombing raids had robbed us of our last healthy nerve. More frequent, more accurate, and deadlier than ever, they seldom missed their intended targets. When enemy scout planes marked a certain square in the sky over our city with their bright yellow flares in the shape of giant Christmas trees, we knew we were in for a heavy bombardment.

The strict federal law of *Verdunkelung* (total blackout) dictated severe punishment for violators. No lights should be visible any place. To prevent enemy airplanes from zeroing in on populated areas, streetlights were no longer turned on at night. These rules, to be observed by all, demanded tightly closed shutters or curtains in houses and anywhere else.

**"The enemy will see your light
Blackout!"**

3

At the first sound of the air-raid siren, Mama, sister Helen with baby Heidi, and I vacated our homes and rushed to the nearest shelter. It was unnerving leaving our front doors unlocked as we hurriedly left, but firefighters needed access to every house or home in case of fire. Incendiary bombs being used by the enemy required immediate action, for they burned fiercely in just seconds. Every household had equipped itself with a big bucket of sand outside the home by the front door. We had learned early on to smother the flames with sand, because water didn't work on these sinister devices.

In order for the basement of our three-story house to be declared a qualified air-raid shelter by the Air Defense warden of our block, we had to make certain changes. The basement of the house had to be reinforced with heavy wooden beams from floor to ceiling. The winter storage supply of coal, firewood, potatoes, and a small amount of apples was pushed into one corner of the cellar to make room for three families with children, plus some emergency equipment like an ax, hammer, shovel, and bucket of sand. Thus the basement was proclaimed a makeshift shelter.

But I remained skeptical in spite of the reinforcements and the window cover made of heavy boards. I never felt safe during air raids and bombardments. I would have preferred the much safer bunkers up the street, especially built by the city with thick, steel-reinforced walls, heavy roofs, and enough room for hundreds of people. Unfortunately even the nearest bunker along the main road was too far from our home.

Late one night, everyone from the house was huddled down in our makeshift shelter during heavy bombardment, with close explosions all around us. A big commotion arose when my sister Helen came rushing in.

"Please, somebody help me extinguish flames in front of our apartment," she pleaded breathlessly. "An incendiary bomb landed on the top floor. The wooden staircase is burning, and I can't handle it by myself."

I don't know who went with her, but it certainly wasn't me. When the chips were down, I turned coward. The earsplitting sound of exploding bombs made me crawl under the old cot, heaping pillows on my head to drown out the sound of detonations. I wanted to protect my face, just in case. A strange thought had crossed my mind: *Even in death, if it does occur, I want my face whole. I don't want it crushed to pulp by tons of cement from a collapsed ceiling.*

After this particularly scary episode, I pleaded with my family to head to a different and maybe safer shelter. A neighbor had told me about the so-called *Felsenkeller,* about an eight-minute walk from our home along the main street. The family finally agreed to go there because of the added safety it most likely would provide.

The last five hundred meters to *Felsenkeller* rose at a slight incline. Fifty-seven steps then led down to a modified wine cellar, a cavernous grotto carved into a granite formation of the elevated landscape. The previously stored wine barrels and racks of bottled wine had been replaced with much more urgent necessities, like old wooden benches, a few chairs, and a couple of cots for the elderly or sick.

The cold and damp cellar required a heavy coat or blanket, but at times we left in such an alarmed hurry that we forgot to grab something to keep us warm. Constant fear gripped our lives, especially when, in total darkness, we were unable to reach the shelter before bombs began to fall. We flung ourselves down close to a wall or into a ditch along the road until after the detonation, and then hurried on before we could hear the eerie, spine-chilling whistle of the next bomb.

I always jumped out of bed at the first sound of the air-raid wail and snatched my warm slacks and sweater from the foot of my bed, without worrying about makeup or neatly combed hair. All I knew was that I had to get the hell out of the house and head for the shelter.

I grabbed my little niece Heidi out of her crib in my sister's room, wrapping her in a blanket while my sister and my mother readied themselves.

"Helen, I'm ready to go. I'm taking Heidi with me."

"Yes. Please hurry. Do you have her blanket?"

"Yes."

"We'll follow as soon as I can get Mama ready."

Mama couldn't manipulate the three flights of stairs too well in total darkness and therefore needed the help of my older sister.

I rushed downstairs, knowing each of the many steps by heart. Racing down the staircase, I juggled Heidi while pulling on the rest of my clothing. With shoes in hand, I landed barefoot at the bottom of the stairs. Tenants living on the lower floors ran ahead of me.

The landlord, who had lost one of his legs years earlier, was waiting in his rickety old pull cart, a makeshift wooden contraption with four rubber wheels and a flimsy handle. Sometimes I grabbed the shaft with my free hand and helped pull him up the street until his wife and daughter could take over. Everybody tried to be as helpful as possible; we were all in the same boat, struggling to survive this madness heaped upon us.

However, I must admit, my first concern was for my year-old niece and myself. My sister and Heidi still resided with us until their evacuation at a later date to a much safer countryside. Months later, after the air raids and destruction had reached their peak, young mothers with small children would be evacuated by order of the government and placed with farm families in outlying suburbs.

I got Heidi safely down the fifty-seven steps into this large, damp, and cold refuge, illuminated with just a few oil lamps. The place filled up fast with upset and tired folks from the neighborhood. They settled on the wooden benches along the walls. I sat somewhere in the corner, away from the stone steps with their terribly cold downdraft. Keeping my eye on the entrance, I waited for the safe arrival of Mom and Sis, holding two more seats for them on my bench. As soon as they arrived, I turned the sleepy bundle of the lovely blonde girl into her mother's arms. Little Heidi eventually fell back asleep.

The murmur of hundreds of voices buzzed among the unhappy cries of small children who had only minutes before abruptly awakened from a sound sleep. Our hearts pounded as the bombs exploded nearby. As we huddled in the confined space, many covered their ears. Others nervously sat and prayed with tightly shut eyes. Everybody anxiously waited for the "all clear" signal, which often took a couple of hours.

When that signal finally came, we went back to our homes and beds and hoped to get a bit more sleep, if for no other reason but that we were absolutely exhausted.

Despite our loss of sleep, we, the young and middle-aged still in the workforce, were required to report for work punctually the next morning—unless we had been injured or killed. No other excuse would do, regardless of the circumstances.

Reports about the previous night's raids, when neighboring houses were leveled to the ground and people perished, didn't help make living any easier for those of us who survived. The soot-blackened chimneys that remained stood amid a heap of rubble and the typical smell of burned wood and crushed cement.

Offenbach am Main after an air raid

7

Like defeated warriors, the chimneys represented an ominous memorial of what had once been a happy home, built with great sacrifices, sweat, and tears by a young couple with big dreams about a happy future together. That memorial served as a reminder for the rest of us living in this period of depravation and insanity.

Air Defense wardens patrolling streets

* * *

In the year of 1941, I acquired my first job as a fledgling secretary for the Federal Railroad headquarters in Frankfurt am Main, approximately nine miles from my hometown of Offenbach am Main. I could take a train to and from work; employees of the railroad received free passes. The war at this point was in its second year, and air raids seemed to be increasing.

One morning, after a dreadful air raid interrupted all public transportation, I was forced to ride my old black bicycle the nine miles to work. Dressed in heavy slacks to ward off the chill, I hopped on my bike and pedaled with all my might to report to work on time. I knew government officials might frown on my attire, as it was considered inappropriate for women to wear slacks. (Another unwritten rule: German women must never smoke in public.)

That morning, as I arrived for work, my boss passed me in the hallway. He had one hand on the doorknob to his office when he turned to me and spoke sternly:

"I want to see you in my office in five minutes."

"Yes, sir," I answered with a sudden lump in my throat. *What can Old Sourpuss possibly want to see me about? What have I done this time?* I had had a few minor problems in the past with this elderly high official, who never seemed to smile, no matter what.

A few minutes later, I knocked on his office door and was told to enter. Standing inside the door, I raised my right arm in the required nationalistic salute and said, "Heil Hitler."

Oh, how I hated that damn greeting. We lived in strange times when a friendly *good morning* or *good evening* was no longer considered proper and had been replaced with the nationalistic salute, even within some politically fanatical families.

"Why are you wearing slacks to the office? You know that it is frowned upon as unbecoming the image of a good German woman."

"Sorry, sir. It was necessary for me to ride my bike to work this morning. All public transportation is down after last night's air raid. And it is very cold outside, as you must know. What was I supposed to do?"

He mumbled something and then said, "You are excused."

This entire incident irked me a lot. I did not like the man, and evidently he didn't like me.

*　　*　　*

A year or two prior to the actual start of the war in 1939, shopping for groceries became a problem. More times than not, we would only get half of the amount we had asked for; if we wanted to buy a half a pound of butter, we'd receive only a quarter pound from the storekeeper, and so it went for most other food items.

Everyone was puzzled, but very soon it became clear that this must be the beginning of rationing. Within weeks, the government had issued ration tickets for food, clothes, underwear, shoes, coal, wood, and—last but not least—for gasoline.

The daily food intake allowed to us shrank to a mere 800 to 1,000 calories, sometimes even less. People turned to bartering, if they had something to barter with. City folks used extra bedsheets, blankets, shoes, or even clothes to obtain farmers' potatoes, vegetables, home-baked bread, or—if especially lucky—a sausage or a piece of meat.

During the postwar years of 1945–1948, I was employed right in my hometown. I got around more than my mother, who was strictly a stay-at-home housewife. It became second nature to me to keep an eye out at all times for people lining up in front of a store, especially a food store. If I spotted a line of people there, I stopped long enough to question someone standing in line.

"What's available at the store today? Are ration tickets needed?" If tickets were required, I rushed home, since my mother kept track of them.

"Mama, at Müller's bakery, customers are standing in line. Do we still have ration tickets for bread? I could go there right now. I was told a shipment of flour came in."

Mother reached for the small folder she kept in a kitchen drawer, checked the remaining ration tickets for this particular week, and handed some to me, together with a couple of coins to cover the purchase.

"Get some flour with the bread tickets. We have enough bread for the next two days. If I save the butter for all of us from this week's ration, I could probably bake a small cake for Sunday."

One week's ration of butter per adult was fifty grams—about the size of a square pat of butter as it was customarily served in restaurants years later.

In a great hurry and with required ration tickets in hand, I headed back to the bakery to stand in line, hoping to get whatever I could before the storekeeper's supply ran out.

Ration tickets for margarine, oil, or lard

At the end of the war, in the postwar years of 1945–1948, *one week's ration* per person was as follows: 3.5 ounces of meat, 3.5 ounces of bread, 4.5 ounces of flour, 2 ounces of lard or shortening, 3.5 ounces of jam, 2 ounces of cheese and cottage cheese, 5 pounds of potatoes, and 1 egg. We considered this a generous portion in comparison to the cutbacks that followed a few weeks later.

Many times during this critical period, I pedaled my bike after work about fifteen miles to the old village of Dietzenbach to visit friends living on a small farm. They often could spare a couple of pounds of potatoes or a loaf of farmer's bread, which was far superior to store-bought bread. *Farmer's bread: how absolutely delicious.*

Mother always appreciated a little extra food for our family of four, but at the same time, she worried about my lonely bike trips. Quite often I couldn't make it back home until 11:00 p.m. The longest stretch toward home took me through a desolate, dark, wooded area, but as I recall now, I was never afraid. Now that the war had ended, I felt more sure of myself and faced life head-on.

Also, since this former national socialist state of ours definitely had become a police state, crime had reached an all-time low. One could walk the streets of the city at midnight, feeling relatively safe. Punishment for crimes committed during the war years always were harsh and swift. For instance, if caught stealing during an air-raid, the culprit could be shot and killed on the spot by patrolling security police. Everybody was aware of such drastic but necessary measures.

* * *

Army Communiqué[1]

August 25, 1944: US troops and General de Gaulle of the French Exile Government move into Paris, formerly occupied by German troops.

October 20, 1944: Allied troops under the command of General Omar Bradley,* First Army, break into Germany and take Aachen. It is the first German city on the border of Belgium that must surrender.

* * *

---

[1]   Army Communiqués describe major events taking place during the war. We, of course, had no knowledge of the events at the time. They are included after the fact and are intended to give the reader a point of reference.

***Note:** Years later, working for the American forces as a secretary-interpreter-translator at V Corps headquarters in the IG Farben Building, Frankfurt am Main, I met General Omar Bradley—in a manner of speaking.

A group of sergeants from my office invited me to go on a coffee break to the Rotunda, a circular building behind the thousand-office main building. As we approached the door, a contingent of high-ranking officers was leaving. All of the men in my group stopped for a snappy salute while I gave a big smile to the general in front, who held the door open for me.

"Good morning, young lady. Please go ahead," the officer said. When I saw the four stars on his shoulder patch, I recognized him as a high-ranking general.

Flustered, all I could say at that moment was a polite "Thank you, sir."

Only afterward did I learn from the sergeants in my group that General Omar Bradley himself had held the door open for me. Wow!

2

DRAFT TO SERVE

Within a couple of years after the start of the war, the German government issued a draft for all men between the ages of sixteen and sixty, able to bear arms, to the so-called *Volkssturm.* The slogan read, *"Um Freiheit und Leben,"* For Freedom and Life.

"For Freedom and Life"
Depicts young man and sixty-year-old

Those draftees were to fill in the gap left by the men serving on several fronts of fighting. The younger of the draftees served as manual laborers doing whatever was needed, such as digging trenches, while the older men filled jobs for the war machine. None were actually sent to the front.

At that point in time (1941–1942), the workweek for the workforce at home increased to sixty hours, and all vacations were canceled. Also, all cultural life stopped, but the government allowed cinemas to remain open. The newsreels that preceded every movie brought to the forefront the heroic struggle and victorious advance of the German forces, but seldom presented the other side of the war story.

In 1941 I had applied for a job at the Federal Railroad headquarters, Frankfurt am Main, *Reichsautobahn Department* (Department Autobahn), and was assigned to the personnel office. I heard that employees in key positions at the railroad had been spared from the draft. However, more and more of my young male colleagues were called to service and bid us good-bye. Many of them were never to return, instead paying the ultimate price: their sacrifice *for the Fatherland*. As one of the local newspapers put it, "The loss of lives with all its pain and suffering is but one of the many cruelties of war."

Finally the government announced that women, too, would be drafted for service. The armaments industry routinely used women in various jobs starting in 1942. It wasn't at all unusual to see female security personnel in factories, female air-raid wardens at public buildings, or female streetcar conductors and drivers. Women also worked as conductors on trains, and many who were highly qualified were placed as engineers on locomotives.

But by 1944, manpower shortages forced the Reich (German empire) to look toward its female population to fill out its ranks, especially in antiaircraft defense units. Male personnel had manned FLAK antiaircraft guns and searchlights up until then. However, government officials felt that young strong women could operate searchlights, while FLAK definitely needed literal manpower to operate the heavy guns. Searchlight batteries worked in close proximity with FLAK batteries. A battery was the smallest unit in a regiment.

Beginning in August 1944, the Reich Labor Service assigned women to operate searchlights, usually under the command of a male corporal or sergeant of the Luftwaffe (air force), to light up the sky at night during enemy plane attacks. They searched for and held planes in their strong beams to enable the FLAK to zero on the target and possibly shoot down a bomb-carrying Allied plane before it unloaded its deadly cargo on heavily populated areas or important industrial regions of Germany.

Rumors about the draft of women into military service circulated for months. I had the feeling my days as a civilian were numbered. Personal matters were never a consideration, and a draft from the nationalistic government could never be refused. This, then, would be my second draft.

*   *   *

Once before, in the fall of 1940, at age eighteen, I had been drafted to the Reichsarbeitsdient, a state labor service organization. For a period of six months, I was forced to leave my first job as a young clerk with the Autobahn Department. It made me very unhappy, because it also meant a long separation from my first love, a young upcoming boxer with a promising future.

*   *   *

The labor service—Reichsarbeitsdienst, or RAD for short—had been founded years earlier with its twofold mission: draft young people to serve the government in predesignated jobs while at the same time teaching military-style discipline. Temporarily, university students, both male and female, were excluded. All others had to go wherever the draft papers stated they must go.

The RAD drafted men at age seventeen and eighteen throughout the country for various jobs requiring manual labor. Their most important tool was symbolized on their shoulder patch, which depicted a spade in a wreath of sheaves of rye with the black swastika prominently centered underneath in a white circle on a red background. During parades the spade was cradled in the left arm with the shaft resting on the left shoulder. The spick-and-span shovels moved in rhythm with the tramping of the boots. The shiny metal parts reflected the rays of the sun in a display of gold and silver.

Reichsarbeitsdienst, or RAD, prepared to march

As the war progressed and escalated, these young men, now between eighteen and nineteen years of age, transferred automatically into the military service at the completion of their one-year RAD commitment.

Young women, however, were to serve as domestics in underprivileged farming households. The final destination of our group of fifty RAD girls was a small, out-of-the-way village high in the Austrian Alps. (Austria had been annexed to the Third Reich of Germany in 1938.)

RAD camp in Hittisau, Austria

**RAD compound: dormitory on left opposite
mess hall, kitchen, and laundry**

Our camp was located approximately three thousand
feet above sea level, at the foot of a mountain that ascended
another thousand feet behind us. The entire RAD compound
consisted of eight wooden structures of various sizes, laid out
in a perfect square on a barren piece of land that was devoid
of grass, flowers, bushes, or trees, but sprinkled with rocks.

21

Every morning at the crack of dawn we raised the swastika flag in a solemn ceremony at the flagpole in the center of the compound. The mess hall, laundry room, and showers stood to one side of the flagpole, while four dormitories were situated at the opposite side. In between sat a smaller building containing living quarters for our four RAD leaders, as well as one larger room serving as a sick bay.

Shortly after our arrival in camp, the first snow fell. It wasn't long before we struggled to get from one side of the camp to the other, slogging through several feet of snow with extreme difficulty. An early detail of six girls was assigned to clear the snow-covered path every morning.

Snow-shoveling detail around flagpole

Another 7:30 a.m. ritual was barefoot calisthenics in the snow. I hated this crazy idea, which was meant to toughen us up. Surprisingly, no one got sick.

Each dormitory housed twelve girls. In the corner of the room stood a small potbelly stove, and our neatly organized lockers lined one wall. Stacked bunks, equipped with straw sacks as mattresses and horse blankets for covers, filled up the room.

Our usual work clothes consisted of a medium-blue dress, a red kerchief to cover our hair, and a brown cardigan for cold days. In addition, we received the regular RAD uniform of a mustard-colored jacket, a skirt of the same color, an off-white blouse with swastika buttons, and an ugly brown, floppy hat to complete the outfit. Girls who enjoyed skiing were offered warm ski pants as well as heavy ski boots, and on weekends we could ski around the neighborhood. That part I loved very much. I had brought my own skis from home, as permitted according to the draft papers, but I had no other necessary equipment.

By order of our top leader, my first assignment as domestic was at a public-school cafeteria in the next village, several miles away. Three feet of snow blanketed the entire area, and the road sloped all the way downhill. I covered the distance to the school on skis in less than fifteen minutes—which allowed me another twenty minutes of skiing practice near school grounds before reporting to work at the designated time. I definitely enjoyed that part.

In this particular area, fairly high in a mountainous region, the children had an all-day school program during wintertime. Most of them arrived on skis, even at age six or seven. They had time off during summer, when many worked in the fields with their families. The government therefore set up a regular free lunch program during the winter, and each child received a nourishing, substantial meal.

"Believe me," explained the pleasant, rotund lady cook, wrapped in a huge chef's apron, "these kids get a better meal here in school than what they have at home. There are no rich farmers in this part of the country. Most of them barely make ends meet for their large families."

Several girls from camp complained to our leaders about unpleasant working conditions at their assignments. For instance, the custom of the entire family eating out of the cooking pots placed in the middle of the kitchen table, a common practice among poor farmers, was totally strange to us. Our leadership therefore requested that all farmers employing an *Arbeitsmaid* must provide a separate dinner plate for them. Still, several of the girls carried sandwiches for their lunch from the camp kitchen to offset totally unsanitary conditions at their work assignments.

The German government financed the cost of household service for all of the impoverished farmers, and we, the actual laborers, were paid in cash every ten days at the rate of twenty-five Pfennig per day (roughly converted: eighteen cents)—barely enough for toothpaste, a bar of soap, or postage stamps to mail a letter home.

Under the labor-service rules, we were considered domestics and not permitted to work in the fields or stables of any farmers. Being a city girl, I wouldn't have done too well pitching manure—or, for that matter, milking a cow. At least I knew on which end to find the cow's udder.

Our tour of duty lasted exactly six months, but seemed much longer to each of us. After the completion of our service, we returned home by train at the end of March in the following year, 1941.

The war by now was in its second year, and the effects of warfare were more painfully perceived at home than in the out-of-the-way village high in the Austrian Alps. In spite of this, everyone was more than happy to be with their families again.

I returned to my previous job, since a new special law required employers to hold jobs open for their former employees upon return from a draft. Consequently, my job at the Autobahn Department in Frankfurt am Main was available.

*   *   *

In the middle of the month of October 1944, I found my dreaded official draft notice in the mail upon returning home from work. The draft was for service with a searchlight battalion. I had been instructed to report to the Frankfurt railroad station, platform 8. The final destination was to be Leipzig, a large town in the eastern part of Germany, 320 miles from my home in the west. *Well, here we go again!*

I disliked this call to duty passionately, but I knew in my heart nothing could be done against an order by our dictatorship government. With a healthy amount of stoicism, I would see it through, just like a million other members of the armed forces in the great, or not-so-great, war machine.

My mother took the news very hard; she was upset to have to let me go, too. I was the youngest of her four children. My two older brothers, Otto (age thirty-seven) and Hans (age twenty-four), had been drafted several years earlier and at that point in time were on the Russian front amid aggressive combat. My departure would leave only my older sister, Helen, and her young daughter, Heidi, at home with Mom.

The time came to pack my little cardboard suitcase with a few necessities. I didn't want to break into tears at the last minute, so I said a fast good-bye to my mother and sister, and off I went to catch streetcar 16, which took me to the south entrance of the main railroad station of Frankfurt—platform 8, our assembly point.

With my draft notice in hand, I reported to the group of military personnel in charge. Several hundred young women, each clutching a bag or suitcase, had arrived ahead of me. They stood around, talking in small groups. None of them looked very happy, except for a few younger volunteers—seventeen- and eighteen-year-olds who seemed gung ho to serve the Fatherland.

We heard the command to board the train and piled into the compartments. A small contingent of military personnel was to accompany us. Everybody scrambled for a halfway decent seat on the already crowded train. The accommodations left many sitting on the floor or standing in the aisle until, hopefully, a seat would become available.

The platform stationmaster in his blue uniform and red cap, stationed toward the end of the train, shouted, "All aboard!"

He lifted his handheld signal, and the engineer immediately engaged the drive shaft of the powerful locomotive, straining under the weight of many cars. Slowly the wheels turned, and the engine, with a threatening hiss, released a stream of thick grayish-white steam into the air, which drifted upward to mingle with the clouds.

The train pulled out of the main station, and at that moment, I felt a sharp pain in my heart. I looked around teary-eyed as the very familiar area of Frankfurt and its surroundings slowly disappeared in the distance.

How long will it be until I return? How much more destruction will the city bear in further bombing raids? How many more people will be killed? There was no immediate answer to all my questions. *Only time will tell, and it is futile anyway for me to worry about situations I can't change.*

With a deep sigh, I wiped the tears away and turned to the young women in the compartment with me.

"Hey, where are you from?" asked the young woman sitting directly across the way.

"Offenbach, on the other side of the Main River. And you? Did you have far to travel?"

"No, I'm from the Taunus Mountain region, north of Frankfurt."

"I got up very early in order to report to the assembly point on time," another girl interjected into the conversation. "I come from Egelsbach and walked a good distance from my house to our train station. I'm tired, and I need to catch up on some sleep."

She sounded angry. Could she possibly be as unhappy about the draft as I was?

Abruptly she wrapped her jacket tightly around her shoulders, leaned back in her seat, and closed her eyes. Several of us engaged in idle conversation. But in spite of the triviality of our talk, I got the distinct feeling that many of the young women were unhappy about the draft, just as I was. We never dared to express it in so many words for fear of being overheard and reported.

An unwritten rule demanded that we keep our tongues in check and only exchange general information when talking to total strangers. These were difficult times, when brother turned against brother, or a young son would turn in his own father to the authorities for a political slip of the tongue. A disparaging remark against the dictatorship government could prove costly and get you arrested. Over all these years, one very important slogan had been hammered into all of our young heads: "Caution—enemy listening," which to me meant that the enemy could be living under the same roof with me, waiting for a chance to turn me in. It referred to so-called traitors, people who opposed the Nazi regime and possibly listened to any conversation, and who also might be dealing with foreign governments.

Feind hört mit
"Enemy listening"

*　　*　　*

Ilsa Fanchin

Army Communiqué

In October 1944, Soviet troops entered Eastern Prussia, Germany.

Germans are fighting more vigorously than ever, defending their homeland.

The Third Army under General Patton is preparing an offensive on the southern border of Germany.

* * *

3

MY FAMILY

The monotone chugging of the train to Leipzig almost lulled me to sleep, but my brain worked overtime and kept me from dropping fully into slumber. Thinking of home, I couldn't help wondering how my mother felt at this moment, after my hasty departure to join the war.

All kinds of memories crept to the surface as I recalled many of Mama's stories about her life as a young woman and how she suffered during WWI (1914–1918) while my father served in the armed forces somewhere in the trenches of France. For four years, she had the monumental job of being the sole support of two small children: my oldest brother, Otto, and my sister, Helen. In addition, and under adverse and trying circumstances, she held down a part-time job to earn much-needed extra money.

After Germany's defeat and the war's end in 1918, Papa picked up the pieces of his life and resumed his career in business management. A few years later, my brother Hans was born, and I entered the world two years after Hans.

Those years after WWI must have been exceptionally harsh. Deprivation everywhere, including a drastic food shortage, added to the misery and pain overall. A period of lean years followed due to a failing economy, as Germany had been burdened with enormous reparations as dictated by the Treaty of Versailles of the foreign powers France and England. As a direct result came inflation when the *Reichsmark* lost its value. As money came into her possession, Mom had to spend it the same day for necessities, because it could have devalued substantially by the very next day.

In 1918, a loaf of bread cost as much as two hundred thousand *Reichsmark* and easily reached twenty million *Reichsmark* in the days to follow. The country was in the grip of political unrest, anarchy, and poverty—but finally, the birth of the Weimar Republic in the year 1919 seemed to ease matters.

Inflation money

*   *   *

September 1, 1939: There was no official declaration of war by the leader of the Deutsche Reich (German empire). Instead, the invasion of Poland that day by German troops was masqueraded as a necessary retaliation against alleged atrocities by Polish soldiers against German subjects still residing in the formerly Free State of Danzig and the so-called Polish Corridor. Prior to WWI they had been part of the German empire.

Officially the German word *Krieg* (war) was not allowed in any German publications at that time. However, afterward, this so-called retaliation was always commonly referred to as *Blitzkrieg,* a war fought with lightning speed.

The Führer had hoped that this retaliation against Poland would avoid the interference of other world powers. However, on September 3, 1939, the foreign minister of Great Britain handed an ultimatum to Hitler to end the invasion of Poland or suffer the consequences. The same day, an ultimatum by France followed. Hitler allegedly was stunned, but did not back off. This, then, was the outbreak of WWII.

Dad did not live to see the start of the war because he had passed away several years earlier. But during the last years of his life, he many times predicted another global war in the making.

All his life he had been a staunch social democrat. He had witnessed the birth of the Weimar Republic (1919) and the installation of its first *Reichspräsident*, Friedrich Ebert. My father never saw eye-to-eye with the concept of national socialism. As a freelance journalist for a local social democratic newspaper, the *Offenbacher Abendblatt,* he lost his job when the paper was forced to close in 1933 by order of the new regime. Unwilling to join the National Socialist Party in 1933, the year the *Führer* came to power, he couldn't find another job because party members were always hired ahead of nonmembers.

Within a very short span of time, my family was forced to go on welfare. But in spite of that, my father steadfastly refused to become a party member. Many a time in the middle of 1933, Dad and I walked downtown to the soup kitchen, where we could get a pot of soup free of charge, provided we brought our own containers. Mama always stayed home; she just couldn't face the long line of unemployed and impoverished.

At that point in time, the long-winded, bombastic speeches of the *Führer* were the order of the day, followed by rhetoric pomposity from his propaganda minister, whose extremely small stature belied his eloquence. Radios blared everywhere, people all intently listening to the promises of the VIP members of the new regime, some skeptical and others enthusiastic and hopeful.

"All of Germany listens to the Führer with the
Volksempfänger" **(radio)**

Dad, very much immersed in politics, felt the need to keep informed, but we didn't own a radio. Consequently, with the very few *Reichsmarks* he struggled to save over the years, he bought a small radio on an installment plan, a so-called *Volks-Empfänger* (*Volk* = nation; *Empfänger* = receiver). This well-built, inexpensive radio was affordable to the average worker and enjoyed by all.

The *Volksempfänger* was in a way the forerunner of the *Volkswagen*.

My family was happy with the new radio. Dad listened to politics, Mom to classical music, and Hans and I to special programs designed for children. We no longer had to press our ears to the wall of our neighbor's apartment when their radio was turned loud enough to let us catch bits and pieces through the partition of a wall.

More than ever, Dad opposed the regime, and the family endured hardships caused by his obstinate and justified

34

opposition to joining the NSDAP Party, including his continued joblessness.

Shortly after the election in 1933, *allegedly* won by the Nazi Party, two storm troopers picked Dad up at our apartment. As an enemy of the ruling party, he was required to work somewhere in the streets of our town, cleaning off graffiti, posters, and slogans left by at least eleven various political parties prior to the election.

I remember exactly what he told Mom: "Lay out my best suit. I wish to appear well dressed to fit the occasion." I thought this funny, since he only had *one* suit.

Another time, two SA (Sturm Abteilung) men in their brown shirts showed up with an order to search our residence for a hidden pistol reportedly in Dad's possession. He assured the troopers he didn't have a pistol stashed away. One of the SA men did not believe him; however, the other man did, as he happened to be Dad's nephew, my cousin Horst. No search took place, because Horst trusted the word of his uncle.

The truth came out much later: Dad didn't have a pistol hidden in our home, but instead it was buried, securely wrapped in oily cloth, in our little garden plot on the edge of town. I never really knew why Dad had a pistol.

Leaders of the newly founded BDM, Bund Deutscher Mädchen (League of German Girls), taught national socialism in classes between social gatherings, and *all* girls were expected to join by the age of ten. Because of Dad's anti-nationalistic beliefs, he never allowed me to join. However, since the majority of my classmates belonged to the BDM, I felt at times I wanted to join, just to do whatever they did during their meetings, although I was not interested in politics at my young age. Members exhibited a kind of Girl Scout camaraderie that appealed to me. Girls who were not members of the youth movement were required to go to school for half a day on Saturdays and take social science and biology classes, while members of the BDM hiked with their leaders or participated in sport events or picnics.

The start of WWII slowly but surely broke my little family apart, along with millions of other families throughout Germany. Mama again faced another world war alone.

Me, Heidi, Helen (Leni), Mama, and Hans

*   *   *

My oldest brother, Otto, served in the German armed forces from day one of the war. By the time of my induction in the fall of 1944, he already had been reported missing in action. Some time after that, my mother received a preprinted postcard via the Red Cross of Switzerland, a neutral country. The spaces on the card had been filled in by my brother (or at least it looked like his handwriting), confirming he was a prisoner of war in Russia.

Shortly before Christmas that same year, while I was in training at the camp near Leipzig, my mother wrote to me, "According to the Swiss Red Cross, Otto is alive and a POW in Russia. We have to wait and see if and when he will be released to return home. His wife and children anxiously await further news. It certainly will not be a very Merry Christmas for any of us."

At the war's end in May 1945, the Russian government did not allow their German war prisoners to be released like most POWs of other powers. Those who eventually made it back to their homes in Germany years later were broken in body and spirit. Many had been brainwashed, just like my brother appeared to have been.

In the summer of 1948, three years after the war's end, Otto finally came home. We learned about his confinement deep inside Siberia after he was captured by Russian forces on the outskirts of Moscow. His infantry unit had fallen behind the German tank division and was then cut off by Russian troops and incarcerated.

"From that point on, all hell broke lose," Otto said. "The Russians took their ire out on us for what they endured. They shipped us by trucks farther east, as close as approximately 320 miles from the Manchurian [Chinese] border. We were forced to work in a salt mine and barely survived on a daily ration of borscht, a beet/vegetable soup served with hard crusted bread."

"Why are your front teeth missing?"

"They were kicked in by a Russian soldier. Early every morning, my group of POWs lined up outside the entrance to the mine while one Russian counted the prisoners. He automatically gave the title of foreman to every twenty-second man, and that foreman was responsible for his crew and the nominal output of the production quota. If the quota wasn't reached, the guards beat the foreman. During my turn as foreman, the Russian soldier in charge kicked in my front teeth.

"Years later," Otto continued, "when I was offered a deal by some Russian bigwig, I grabbed the chance for release. I took the oath to work for the idea of communism in my home country—attend party meetings, distribute communistic literature, and rally 'round the red flag. Without blinking an eye, I gave my oath. I wanted to get home to my wife and six children."

We finally understood. Nobody in the family would or could ever criticize his actions. We all agreed that under the same circumstances, we probably would have done the same.

*   *   *

My second brother, Hans, fought with the first German troops to invade Poland on September 1, 1939, in the *Blitzkrieg*. It took less than a month to practically wipe the country of Poland off the map, as it became divided between Germany and Russia. At that point in time, it was common belief that everyone would leave it at that, ending the conflict. Instead, it was only the beginning of WWII as the German forces steadily advanced onto Russian soil.

Hans, too, ended up in Russia. During a bitterly cold winter, he suffered from frostbite in both feet. He was subsequently evacuated to a military hospital in Hannover, Germany, for possible amputation of his feet.

When this news reached Mama, she asked me to try to take a few days off from work and go to the hospital to get firsthand information as to Hans's condition. I requested a few days' leave and a railroad pass from my employer and headed to Hannover. Upon arrival, I found my way to the army hospital and to the right hospital room.

Happy to see me, Hans wanted to know all about things back home. The Feldpost, or military mail, had had difficulty getting through, leaving him totally in the dark about friends and family. Our conversation was lively and animated when suddenly, and with a big smile, he interrupted our conversation and poked his feet out from under the covers.

"Look, I still have them both! I would never have given my consent for amputation. I'd rather die than be without feet."

"And how do you feel now, Hans?"

"Pretty good, considering. On cold days, I constantly have a tingling sensation in my feet. The doctor tells me it will always be that way. But that's nothing when you consider the alternative. I'm grateful my doctor found a special treatment to save my feet."

A few months later, Hans was released from the hospital and ended up with the German forces in Italy, instead of being returned to his outfit in Russia.

By the winter of 1943, the American forces already occupied a large part of Italy. From January to May 1944, bitter and deadly fighting raged on between German and American troops in the area where an old Italian monastery, Monte Cassino, was situated on a prominent spot high in the Italian Alps.

Monte Cassino

According to confidential reports released after the war, the German command secretly occupied the monastery, an excellent strategic location that overlooked the entire valley. The German military erroneously believed that American forces would not attack or bomb a monastery, but this military gamble did not pay off.

A report from the German War Department read,

"German troops held their position at Monte Cassino against great odds."

*　　*　　*

Army Communiqué

May 25, 1944: The fall of Monte Cassino followed the most savage fighting of the Italian campaign. The Americans broke the spine of the Nazi defense by punishing the fortress with its largest and most powerful mobile gun, the 240-mm howitzer.

*　　*　　*

Within a short span of time, Hans, embedded with the Signal Corps in Italy, intercepted messages in English over his field telephone. He knew then it was time to retreat, since defeat seemed inevitable. But before any action could be taken, the entire corps was captured by American troops.

Hans and fifty other German POWs were loaded onto a big 2.5-ton truck covered with an olive-drab tarp. Through the grapevine, the prisoners heard rumors that the truck was headed for the infamous POW camp of France, somewhere on the other side of the German border. (Early on, French POW camps acquired a bad reputation among German soldiers as far as food and the general treatment of POWs were concerned.)

During an emergency truck stop around midnight, Hans recognized the surroundings; they were still on German soil. With the help of one of his buddies, who acted as a lookout, he managed to slip away from the American truck and walked due north to get home.

In the open fields of a partially wooded area, he had a chance encounter with a very sympathetic young farm woman. At first, startled by his sudden appearance out of nowhere, she started to retreat.

"You frightened me for a moment until I recognized your German uniform. Where did you come from this early in the morning?"

"I'm trying to walk home toward Frankfurt," Hans replied. "I've walked half of the night so I would not be detected. I'm exhausted. Do you think I could rest up for a while at your farm? And I hate to ask, but could I have a couple slices of bread? I haven't eaten since yesterday."

She invited him to walk with her to her parents' small farm close by. He washed up and afterward was given a wonderful breakfast of fried eggs, bread, and *Ersatzkaffee* (substitute coffee). To hide the German uniform, the young woman handed him a coat that had formerly belonged to her soldier husband. She also gave him a rake to carry to give the impression of a farmer coming from the field. He accepted the rake plus the bundle of hay tied to the end of it and slung it over his shoulder.

After a short rest, he proceeded on his journey. He finally reached Offenbach after hours of walking and headed for Mother's small apartment, located on the third floor of a building along one of the major roads of town. He rang the doorbell.

Mama answered the door, cautiously opening it as far as the safety chain allowed. Upon seeing her son, she shrieked and with trembling hands removed the chain. Hans caught her in a big hug as her knees crumpled in her excitement.

"Hans, my boy. What a surprise! You came home. You are well. Come in. You must be exhausted. Sit down at the kitchen table. I'll fix you something to eat."

Mama pushed him ahead of her to the small, but tidy kitchen, where she immediately put on a kettle of water to make a pot of tea. She served part of her own rations without hesitation: a bit of leftover soup as well as a few slices of luncheon meat and bread.

"And what about you, Mama?"

"I'm not very hungry, Hans," she answered. "You must eat, and then tell me what has happened. Where did you really come from? No, no," she interrupted herself. "You sit and eat. We'll talk later. I'm so happy you are finally home. Thank the Lord."

For fear of capture, Hans decided to hide away temporarily in my little summerhouse, a one-room wooden structure near a small lake in the countryside. Mom packed as much food as she could spare neatly into a satchel while Hans changed into old civilian clothes—which were now much too large, because he had lost a lot of weight.

He bicycled the long route through a wooded area to avoid detection by any member of the occupational forces.

*　　*　　*

My older sister, Helen, and her young daughter, Heidi, still lived with Mom and me in our apartment. Helen's husband, Heinz, was fighting on the Russian front. The living arrangement was beneficial for both parties; neither side had to cope alone, and we could share the living expenses.

In due time, Helen was also recruited by the government, but luckily her assignment was an eight-to-five job in an ammunition factory right in our town of Offenbach, where she could be home at night with Mama and her baby girl. But even in that particular job, she lived in constant fear of explosions and other accidents. Many a time she rushed home extremely upset.

"Again today, there was another explosion in the gunpowder room that injured two workers," she told us one day. "One woman had to be taken to the emergency clinic, and the second one was treated by the plant nurse. At times I'm just scared as hell. And to think we manufacture ammunition to kill *other* human beings."

*　　*　　*

Helen's husband, Heinz, had left for the Russian front at the very beginning of the war. Much later I read portions of a letter written by him and learned he had volunteered for that assignment. This absolutely blew my mind; only the most politically fanatic or those with a death wish *volunteered* for the Russian front.

According to information received from the War Department, Heinz was killed on his thirty-second birthday in March 1945, shortly before war's end in May that same year. Prior to his death, during a short leave of absence from the army, Heinz saw his baby girl for the first and only time when she was twelve months old.

His family took his death very hard. Heinz's father had served four years as an officer during World War I. To me, the old man seemed the epitome of an officer of the old guard: the well trained, disciplined Prussian officer of Kaiser Wilhelm fame. His son's death hit him hard, but it was just another ultimate sacrifice for the Fatherland.

Heinz's mother, a gentle, sweet and soft-spoken woman, shed many tears over her son's untimely death. How much sorrow and how much pain can a mother's heart possibly hold without breaking?

The loss of life affected everyone, including immediate and extended family, friends, and acquaintances. Like circles on the water of a pond spreading from the impact of a stone, the pain spread rapidly, sparing no one.

4

INDUCTION

I must have fallen asleep after all on the train to Leipzig, but the sharp jolt of the train coming to a stop at the main station woke me. Everyone piled out of the railroad cars, which had been specially reserved for inductees. We boarded army trucks and headed to a red, four-story brick army barracks in another part of town.

Our military-style accommodations in one wing of the huge barracks were not exactly first-class. We shared the mess hall with army men, which accounted for all the whistles and shouts whenever our group of new female inductees entered. The wing on the third floor was reserved only for female draftees—strictly off limits to all men.

In the days to follow, the usual medical tests were administered in one of the larger rooms upstairs by a team of military doctors and nurses. Required to stand in a straight line, about twenty young females at a time waited to be examined by two or three doctors. The girls were of all walks of life: pretty and not so pretty; fat and skinny; tall and short; flat-chested or absolutely needing the support of a good bra. But bras were not allowed at this particular examination.

Uncomfortable standing in line practically stark naked, I left my slip pulled over my breasts, straps hanging to the side, and stepped forward for my turn.

"Get that goddamn slip off, girl," the doctor yelled.

I dropped it immediately in a gesture of defiance and humiliation.

Several large cabinets divided the huge examination room. A nurse handed each girl a paper cup with instructions to step

47

behind the dividers and give a specimen. I carefully tiptoed around the many puddles already formed on the floor and made my contribution.

Reichsarbeitsdienst (RAD) uniforms had been issued prior to the physicals. Sadly, I had packed my own personal clothes into my cardboard suitcase. As of that moment, my navy-blue blazer and light-gray skirt (my pride and joy, so to speak) were replaced by a mustard-colored two-piece uniform and a dingy brown felt hat. The RAD emblem on the uniform jacket sleeve depicted an elongated wreath of sheaves of rye with the black swastika centered in a white circle on a red background. Even the buttons on the off-white uniform blouse bore the imprint of a swastika.

Arbeitsmaid in uniform (me)

I hated everything about this uniform: the fit, the color, the hat, and especially the swastika on the patch. The hat more than anything gave me a pain in the backside. It didn't fit well because I had worn my hair in an upswept style for many years. Now our leader ordered that I wear it in a style "more appropriate" for a labor service member in uniform. Another rule: no makeup of any kind—just plain, wholesome, stouthearted German girls.

I wondered, *Is that the way we are also perceived in foreign countries?*

Years later, at the war's end, my question was in a sense answered.

Stars and Stripes, a daily newspaper printed for the occupational forces in Germany, carried the "Sad Sack" cartoon. Depicted as a pathetic, sad, and simpleminded member of the armed forces, the main character courts Veronika Dankeschön, a hefty German girl always wearing army boots and swastika ribbons tied to her long, blonde braids. Her initials were V. D., meant to be the abbreviation for venereal disease. I found such a cartoon offensive, but at that time, I didn't have the guts to complain to the editor of the American paper.

*   *   *

Concerning makeup, I remember a kind of funny incident during one of the periodic assemblies of the entire battalion—approximately three hundred female soldiers and only twenty-five men—in a wide-open field behind the battalion headquarters. The battalion commander was preparing to give us a pep talk. But before he could even begin his well-rehearsed little speech, our labor service leader called for me and my comrade and friend, Ruth, to step forward. As I took one large step forward, I gave Ruth a quick glance. She seemed as puzzled as I was.

"Fall out and head for the bathroom," the leader commanded. "After you wash the paint off your faces, you may come back."

Our faces turned red, and we hurried toward the headquarters building amid chuckles and laughter from the assembled troops. As we reached the bathroom, I turned to Ruth.

"What was that you said about nobody noticing if we put on a tiny bit of makeup?" I asked.

Ruth shrugged, but her face wore a big smile. "Guess we got caught, huh? I had not counted on old Eagle Eyes."

We both started to giggle as we scrubbed our faces. Minutes later, upon our return to the field, the leader gave us a scrutinizing look before we quietly fell into formation.

* * *

For disciplinary matters, we were under the command of the labor service and wore the RAD uniform. However, for active service on the searchlight in the field, we would be issued the more practical bluish-gray coveralls and caps of the air force.

Within three days after our arrival at the army barracks in Leipzig, trucks transported forty-eight of us new soldiers and one young RAD leader to the small town of Pölzig, a village southwest of Leipzig with a population of approximately 1,200. We unloaded in front of the village theater, a two-story brick building right next to the only local restaurant.

The War Department had requisitioned the theater as temporary quarters for military personnel. The inside had been gutted, and the necessary equipment to house about fifty draftees had been set up.

Consequently, the group of traveling cinematic experts, with their portable projectors and equipment to show movies, were restricted, much to the regret of the villagers. The movies probably had been the biggest and maybe sole entertainment for the farmers in this small village off the beaten track. Although unhappy, the villagers wouldn't dare to complain, fearing reprisals from the government.

With winter approaching, the village's main road, lined with many tall bushes and trees whose bare branches reached skyward, was deserted, except for a few pedestrians and an occasional horse-drawn wagon. Modest little farms and a few two-story apartment houses sprinkled the countryside of large, flat fields as far as you could see.

I had lived and worked in a big city all my life, and I missed the hustle and bustle of cars, buses, streetcars, and motorcycles. Here, I encountered only a few people, horses, and cows on the normally isolated road. I also missed the Taunus mountain range near my home; on a clear day, one could see the top of the Feldberg mountain, a 2,400-foot elevation.

The different and dull landscape in this part of the country depressed me.

5

LIFE IN CAMP

A wide stone staircase on the outside of the theater building led to the large theater room on the second floor, bypassing the ground-floor laundry and storage rooms. Before entering the large hall through the wide double door, we passed a blackout curtain hung on the inside of the door. Eight huge windows—four on each long side of the large room—also had roll-down blackout shades. All doors and windows adhered to the strict regulations of total blackout.

The two potbellied stoves in opposite corners of this spacious room were the only source of heat; however, firewood was in short supply, and we seldom were able to start a fire. More times than not, all of us felt very cold. Those evenings when the potbellies glowed from a good fire, we huddled around the stoves to catch waves of warmth, listening to the crackling of wood and inhaling its aromatic smell of pine sap, birch, or oak. Shortly before the flames died down, with our bodies and pajamas nicely warmed, we hopped into our bunks, drawing the blankets tightly around us to retain some of the pleasant warmth. Soon the chattering of the girls died down with the fire; a few hours of peace, quiet, and sleep followed a normally hectic and busy training day.

Two-thirds of the theater hall functioned as a dormitory. Four long rows of wooden double bunk beds were placed against one of the longer walls underneath the windows, along with our individual lockers. The other third of the room, designated as the mess hall, held a row of heavy wooden tables and benches positioned alongside the opposite wall. The elevated spacious stage with its dark-green curtain dominated one end of the long hall.

A very small kitchen located by the double-door entrance contained the absolute minimum of equipment: a combination woodstove/gas range, a simple shelf with several large pots and pans, and a small counter with drawers containing the cutlery. A small sink in the corner dispensed only cold water.

This huge, cold, dull, and sober room represented our only residence. Here, we worked, ate, slept, and often cried, longing for the comfort of family and home. But most of all, we longed to be away from the hardship of our regimented routine, which left very little time for personal matters.

For the following four to six weeks, the daily schedule remained the same:

After reveille at six a.m., we got ready for a fast cleanup job in the cold downstairs laundry room—which meant we jumped immediately out of our bunks and into the soft, woolen, navy-blue training suits, since we had to hurry down the freezing-cold outside staircase to the laundry room. There, in one corner of the room, a huge copper water basin mounted on a large stone fireplace held enough warm water for all of us (again, subject to the availability of dry firewood). When we had no warm water for our daily cleanup, the only alternative was the cold water faucet.

Three benches along one of the longer walls held several heavy ceramic bowls—a substitute for built-in washbasins—but no tub or shower. In an almost ritualistic scuffle, I fought my daily battle for one of the washbowls and considered myself darn lucky to grab one. Scooping warm water from the copper basin into the bowl at least made a sponge bath possible—although it wasn't as easy as it sounded.

In due time (especially on weekends), I created my own system: I washed my top half, placed the bowl on the floor, and scrubbed my bottom half. However, standing in a relatively small bowl with both feet while washing resembled a balancing act in a circus. It definitely required a lot of practice, even for those who possessed a perfect equilibrium.

To make things worse, several bowls broke within a short time, which left a mere six bowls available for all forty-nine girls. Without a bowl, the only alternative was the cold-water faucet, which possibly shocked you into dreams about a heavenly hot shower (but such luxury simply did not exist). After the morning scrub, I slipped back into my training suit, hurried up the cold outside staircase to the hall, and jumped into the service coveralls with great speed to be ready for fallout and head count.

Our daily schedule was one long game of show and tell, with much to be seen and even more to be heard.

Our RAD labor leader, Miss Klein, was a young brunette of medium build and height. Her room and personal space on the theater's stage overlooked the entire dormitory.

Although she was two years younger than I was, I soon realized that age had nothing to do with rank. With envy I observed that she had the thick stage curtain to hide behind if needed.

Miss Klein outlined the various assignments daily. Whoever drew kitchen detail had the additional job of drawing rations from the quartermaster at battalion headquarters, two miles from camp. A detail of two or three girls was assigned to draw rations, accompanied by one of the neighborhood farmers and his horse-drawn wagon. (The farmers were required to furnish manpower and transportation on a biweekly basis.)

This errand required every bowl, sack, box, and other available container, including our washbowls from the laundry room.

However, occasionally a girl left her underwear soaking in one of the bowls.

"Hey, who has laundry soaking in a bowl downstairs?" a loud angry voice from one of the kitchen staff would call out. "Get it out fast! We need the bowls for rations. Hurry up."

The culprit would sprint downstairs, remove her laundry, wash the bowl with a lick and a promise, and run back upstairs to the kitchen to deliver it.

Trainees on the searchlight left early after a meager breakfast consisting of two slices of bread, jam, and coffee. The bread, called *Kommiss Brot* (*Kommiss* is slang for army), was a square loaf of grayish-brown bread made from various grains with a lot of bran for filler. Many times mold already had formed on the sides of the loaves before they even reached the camp kitchen. If that happened, we scratched it off and ate it anyway, because there wasn't anything else.

Ersatzkaffee was a brew made from toasted wheat germ with chicory added; regular coffee beans could no longer be imported due to the total isolation of Germany. The brew was hot, wet, and brown in color, but the resemblance to coffee ended there; its taste was absolutely awful.

Walking with my group down the road for a training session at the nearest searchlight in the field, I remembered the advice of a sergeant I had encountered weeks earlier at the Leipzig barracks.

"Girl, if you can choose your position on the searchlight, take the machinist job."

"Machinist job?" I answered in total surprise. "But I don't know anything about machines!"

The sergeant assured me my training would teach me the operation of a twelve-cylinder Daimler-Benz motor and everything else required to make the searchlight operational.

"One advantage," he said, "is that the motor equipment is always housed in a small shed to one side of the compound, away from the searchlight. The machinist therefore is protected from the elements. The rest of the crew is out in the trenches and exposed to all kinds of weather."

I took the sergeant's advice and volunteered for the machinist position upon arrival at our first training session. The instructor, a sergeant, appointed me ahead of anybody else. Thus far, I had the title but no experience at all.

The remainder of our training time that day was spent naming the different parts of the searchlight and understanding how it operated. We were admonished to remember it all. Then the sergeant proceeded to demonstrate how a searchlight worked.

At noon we walked back to camp for dinner. Upon entering the mess hall, I spotted our multipurpose washbowls on top of the long row of tables, filled with steaming lumps of potatoes, cabbage, and stew.

When I had seen our washbowls filled with food for the first time, it shocked me and spoiled my appetite. But in due time, hunger surpassed my disgust, and I learned to put up with it. Big metal pitchers filled with skim milk the color of pale blue water graced the table next to the washbowls. Under the rationing system, only small children and very old people were entitled to whole milk.

All of us hurriedly dug in so that we could get a second helping in case there were any leftovers. Soon it was time to return for another training session in the afternoon.

Within the first few hours of training, I understood the disadvantage of a machinist: I had to be the first person in position at any alert, since time was of the essence. The motor needed to be primed and warmed up several minutes before the searchlight crew was in place.

*   *   *

Temperatures had dropped to freezing, which presented a problem for girls in need of a bathroom at night. Our toilet facility (if you could call it such) was clear around the compound, on the opposite side of the building. Even during the day, it was sheer misery to visit that place: a small and dirty little one-holer outhouse for all fifty of us. We had no water to flush, no water faucet to wash our hands, and—worst of all—no toilet paper.

On the way back to the hall, we had to stop at the ground-floor laundry room in order to wash our hands. Probably not everyone bothered. Maybe by the time they reached the laundry room on their return, they had forgotten the whole matter anyway.

But we had better not forget that square piece of newspaper handed out at reveille every morning, because the "biffy" had no toilet paper. At critical times, I put my faith into girls lined up in front of the old, wooden toilet door with its crescent moon at the top. Some of the girls awaiting their turn often had an extra piece of paper to donate.

The days grew shorter, and the chilly north wind brought bitterly cold temperatures. The howling wind and utter darkness of a blackout made nights spooky. Everyone dreaded the long walk to the toilet in total darkness. Soon some of the girls employed an emergency measure. Too scared at night to venture any farther outside the hall than to the top platform of the stone steps, they tinkled right there when nature called. Freezing temperatures at night created slippery steps by morning. On closer inspection of the small garden area near the bottom of the steps, you noticed small frozen piles of human feces, which I dubbed "forget-me-nots." A special detail quickly buried them.

Lina, the girl in the bunk next to me, had yet another bright idea: she acquired a large tin marmalade bucket with a lid, which she used as a chamber pot. We considered this scheme ridiculous and protested the use of the bucket. Several times, Lina made such a racket in the still of the night—the sound seemingly multiplied, reminiscent of a miniature waterfall.

In addition we had to deal with the awful smell.

"What are we going to do about Lina's bucket?" asked Irma, whose bunk was above Lina's. "She claims she has a bladder infection and cannot be expected to go to the outhouse in total darkness and cold weather."

"I feel sorry for her," I said. "But I don't think the use of this smelly bucket is fair to the rest of us. I, too, have it right under my nose and don't like it one bit. What an awful mess we would have if other girls followed Lina's example."

Ruth shuddered in disgust. "Who has the courage to do away with the bucket?"

"I do," I said. "If the rest of you keep Lina occupied, I'll swipe the bucket at the right moment and throw it on the farmer's manure pile next door." End of bucket.

6

UNHAPPY HOLIDAYS

Advent season in Germany starts four weeks prior to the actual Christmas holiday. Tradition requires each home to be decorated with an *Adventskranz,* a wreath made of pine-tree branches and decorated with four red candles, four red ornaments, and red ribbon wrapped around the greenery. Each candle represents one week's time prior to the actual Christmas day.

So, a group of girls from camp scrounged pine-tree branches and fashioned them into a traditional advent wreath. Anni found bright-red ribbon, and Ella donated the four red candles she had received from home. The red ornaments ordinarily on the wreath had to be replaced with four large pinecones, but still, everyone was happy with our little masterpiece.

At Sunday morning breakfast, the candles on the wreath were lit, offering a chance for all of us to reminisce for just a few minutes—each in her own way. However, our hearts felt heavy, and we were all terribly homesick on this particular holiday away from our loved ones.

One morning at reveille, our leader announced, "Listen up, girls. We're going to have a Christmas tree delivered by one of the farmers. It should be here within the next few days. Think about decorations and such. See what you can do."

The news caused quite a stir. Everyone got busy hustling up anything Christmassy to decorate our tree. I collected strips of thin, shiny metal found along the road. It was claimed that enemy airplanes had dropped those as a sonic decoy, preventing correct pinpointing so that FLAK could not shoot down their planes.

Back in camp, I cut the shiny metal into small strips. Voilá! We had tinsel for our tree. Pinecones completely covered with the same thin metal made wonderful ornaments. After the tree was delivered, everyone caught the enthusiasm of this special project. Our mess hall looked like Santa's workshop.

Some girls had received small packages from home with delicious and rare cookies and apples. They sacrificed a few for the decoration of the tree and tied them to the tree branches with ordinary sewing thread. Our sparsely decorated pine tree, adorned with wax candles of various sizes and colors and crowned with a silver star fashioned from the metal of our enemies, represented a masterpiece created in troubled times by troubled souls. The tree remained center stage and for days was the focus of our attention. Peace on Earth!

"*Stille Nacht, Heilige Nacht*"—"Silent Night, Holy Night"—echoed the most revered Christmas song throughout the big hall of our living quarters. On Christmas Eve, we assembled at the foot of the stage, our eyes glued to our tree. The lit wax candles diffused their golden glow, and the unique smell of Christmas filled the air. With heavy hearts, fifty voices belted out songs remembered from childhood. We were by no means a master chorale, but we nevertheless sang with all the fervor we could muster under the circumstances. Many teary eyes seemed to appear in minutes, and after one verse of "*Stille Nacht*," even our voices filled with tears.

On this very special night, all of us wanted more than ever to be home with our families, our sweethearts, and our friends in a familiar environment instead of in a big, cold hall, surrounded by strangers, amid a terrible and costly war.

While sitting in groups beneath the stage, we reminisced about the past in general and other Christmas holidays in particular. We leaned on each other for moral support, dredging up stories from childhood, from before this terrible war—before bombings and before our draft to service. I stared at our makeshift tree and remembered Christmases past.

* * *

My mind drifted to my most vivid memory of Christmas Eve as a child: sitting with the entire family in the cozy and warm parlor, which we used only for special occasions. Fifteen years earlier in my life, my family had resided in a large housing complex consisting of four-story buildings, each housing eight families.

Housing complex in Offenbach am Main
Me (far left) and my friends from the neighborhood

I had plenty of children to play with, and some of my playmates were also my classmates in the nearby school.

Everyone excitedly awaited *Christkind* (Christ-child), who would arrive on the evening of December 24 to bring gifts. Early in my childhood, I was told that *Christkind,* an angelic creature with golden hair, beautiful white wings, and a white, flowing gown, was bringing the gifts on Christmas Eve, accompanied by Santa Claus, her helper. However, I would probably never see them; they had the power to appear and disappear at will and often came through closed windows into rooms while the children slept. They floated away to the next houses in the same manner.

Just a few days prior to the holidays, on a crisp and clear winter morning, Papa prepared to buy our Christmas tree at the market downtown.

"Please, Papa, may I go with you to pick our tree?" I pleaded.

"Can I take her along, Mama?" he asked.

"Yes, go ahead. Maybe Hans would like to go also. Take him along."

Off we went: Papa, my brother Hans, and me. Papa selected our tree very carefully. It had to be "just right," as he put it. Not too tall, not too short, freshly cut, and, most of all, not too expensive, as he was still unemployed and had very little money. He asked the salesman for a few extra pine boughs in case the tree needed a branch here or there to give it a more balanced look.

"Mother Nature does not always produce perfect-looking trees," Papa quipped.

The marketplace buzzed with excitement and people. The Christmas-bazaar stalls, decorated with colored lights and Christmas ornaments, did a brisk business, and the air was laden with the smell of gingerbread, cinnamon sticks, and candied almonds, along with the distinct aroma of ripe apples mixed with the fragrance of fresh pine.

"Papa, may I buy a gingerbread heart for Mama?" Hans asked.

"And Papa, may I buy some candied almonds for us?" I begged.

"I don't have much money left after buying the tree. But here, ten Pfennig for each of you. Hurry up," he said. "We must get home."

Hans and I made our big purchases and quickly returned to Papa. Hans grabbed the light end of the tree, while Papa carried the end with the heavy trunk for the long walk home. I dawdled along, happily munching on my share of candied almonds.

Mama greeted us from the top of the stairs.

"It's a lovely tree, Otto." She nodded and smiled in approval.

Papa stored the tree in a cool place, and we would not see it again until the evening of December 24, Christmas Eve. When dusk enveloped our quiet little world on that day, Hans and I were electrified with excitement and anticipation. Papa rang a handbell, and Mama opened the door to the parlor. Hans and I were finally allowed to stand right inside the door. In awe we glanced at the decorated tree, now in its stand on top of the dining-room table. White wax candles cast a golden light that was reflected by the tinsel and colorful ornaments. The silver star atop shone brightly, as if just having soared down from heaven itself.

Throughout the room, waves of fresh pine scent mingled with the fragrance of apples, oranges, and nuts displayed in a pretty bowl on a side table. The entire family stood by the tree, singing *"Stille Nacht, Heilige Nacht."* We quickly looked around the room with unbridled excitement to spot our individual place where presents were displayed.

"Hans," I whispered, "have you spotted any of your presents yet? I wished for a little doll in a red doll bed, and it is over there in the corner."

"Yes, I think I recognized the large box of an Erector Set over there. That's what I wished for."

After only one verse of the Christmas song, we were allowed to head for our own little niche to play with our presents. In those days, nothing was wrapped in pretty paper. It was too costly for most families, including my own, to buy special paper and pretty bows.

With love and devotion, presents bought days before for all special persons in our lives were exchanged amid excitement, laughter, and happiness. The distinct smell of Christmas included the unmistakable scent from the kitchen, where the traditional Christmas goose already sizzled in the oven.

Bescherung, gift giving, is always on the evening of December 24, followed by the first holiday, December 25, and the second holiday, December 26. Mama served dinner for each holiday at noontime. The typical feast of goose included potato dumplings and sweet-sour cabbage. Mother stuffed the goose with a well-seasoned mixture of ground meat and bread, to stretch it a bit in case guests dropped in unexpectedly. For the afternoon, Mama brought out coffee, along with Christmas *Stollen*, the traditional coffee cake shaped like a long, flat log that contained almonds, raisins, candied lemon, orange peel, and various spices.

As if by sheer magic, when dusk set, it started to snow.

"It's snowing! It's snowing!" my brother shouted.

We cheerfully rushed outside to meet many children of the neighborhood to dance among the snowflakes, which landed on our eyelashes and the tips of our noses. We giggled and twirled around in sheer delight and true Christmas spirit. The gas lanterns along the streets glowed, casting their golden reflection on the snow. Once the snowing stopped, the sky was illuminated with millions of stars, which seemed especially bright this Christmas Eve. *Indeed a silent, holy, and magical night!* What wonderful childhood memories.

$$* \quad * \quad *$$

I had become lost in my daydreams, but an abrupt shout from our leader brought me back to reality and a cold hall.

"Time for supper!" she commanded. "Take your places!"

Supper consisted of the usual bread and cold cuts. I really don't remember what was served that night, nor do I care to. All I wanted was for those holidays to pass quickly so that my heart wouldn't ache any longer. I felt unhappy and missed my family more than ever.

For the following two holidays, we were not required to train on the searchlight, and it seemed as if the war, too, had taken a holiday. We spent most of our free time sitting together for moral support, exchanging stories or writing letters. The break also gave us a chance to take care of laundry and other personal matters. Cards and letters received from home were read and reread, often dozens of times.

Our leader, during a couple of hours of instruction, told us what to expect at the beginning of the new year. We would transfer in small groups of twelve to fourteen into individual searchlight batteries within the vicinity of neighboring villages.

Thus the 234th Searchlight Battalion, with a combined strength of three hundred female soldiers and a total of twenty-five men for supervision and training, was established.

After the holidays, things returned to normal, or what was considered normal in our camp.

One morning at reveille, Miss Klein made an announcement.

"Girls, I will leave for about three days. During my absence, I will put one of you in charge. I expect things to run as smoothly as possible. Ilsa, step forward."

Oh, boy. Now what?

"I want you to take charge of the camp. You know the military agenda, and I'm sure you can handle it. I expect everyone here to cooperate."

I stood at attention.

"Jawohl," (Yes, sir) I answered in the German military style but thought, *Why me? Doesn't she know how much I hate this life, this commitment for the Fatherland, and this whole ideology of* "unser Führer"?

My dad had raised my brother Hans and me with values and ideas that stood in sharp contrast to national socialism. Although very young then, we reasoned he must be right.

I felt unhappy as hell and did not feel honored by this nomination. To oppose orders from the dictatorship regime or to swim against the treacherous current of national socialism had been a surefire death sentence for numerous people in the past few years. To say the least, such oppression could and would make life miserable for any detractor of the regime.

"Learn early on to bend," my dad often had said, "like that proverbial young tree bends in a storm. Make the best of any situation, no matter how unpleasant or inconvenient." Alas! With a stiff upper lip I started running the camp.

For the next few days, everything seemed to go well, and most of the girls were very cooperative. The individual groups assigned to train on the searchlight left on time. The kitchen personnel had their usual job to do, and no problems with food preparation.

Wanting to set a good example, I took the lousiest, dirtiest job and scrubbed the tiny filthy outhouse.

In order not to get too close to the mess, I used a pair of old gloves, a long-handled brush, and a garden hose I borrowed from the proprietor of the restaurant next door. I tried to work off all my pent-up emotion and frustration with feverish scrubbing, all the while wondering how a toilet used by women only could possibly get so filthy dirty. Afterward I felt the need for a thorough cleanup and headed for the laundry room, making my inspection for that particular room at the same time.

The kitchen was my next stop to see what possibly would be needed there. The necessary daily reports for rations and equipment had to be prepared, in addition to other required paperwork. Once before, I had assisted Miss Klein with this type of work and knew what needed to be done.

The troops returned at noon from their training session on the searchlights within our perimeter. Some of the girls were quite excited. They had watched a dogfight between a German Messerschmitt fighter plane and a British Spitfire.

It became second nature for most of us to watch the skies while on duty outside, and many in the group could identify various planes by sight and sound.

Hanna, a rather thin and nervous young woman originally from a small village near my hometown, approached me. (She always seemed to worry about anything and everything.)

"Ilsa, you must check this out," she said anxiously. "We watched a fierce dogfight a few minutes ago. One of the pilots parachuted down, but we couldn't be sure he was from the

German plane. He landed nearby, causing a lot of commotion in the neighborhood and in the restaurant next door." With her voice reaching a crescendo, she added, "What if he is an enemy spy? You're in charge. Go see what this is all about."

I felt I should go to the nearby restaurant and see for myself just what had happened. If nothing else, maybe I could be of help in some way.

I saw a highly agitated pilot in a gray-blue Luftwaffe uniform, part of the harness still on his back and the parachute bundled up by his feet. The insignia on his collar indicated he was a second lieutenant. He evidently had suffered slight injuries. One of the local policemen who happened to be on the premises gave him first aid.

When I tried to explain my presence and offered help, the pilot brushed me off in no uncertain and offensive German language. He was in no mood for idle chitchat.

The innkeeper and his wife told me the policeman would take the injured pilot by motorcycle to the nearest Luftwaffe station.

Returning to camp, I related the story. Hanna and the rest of the girls calmed down. The following day, I reported the incident to our leader upon her return.

"Thank you for the report, Ilsa. I will have a talk with the people next door for verification. An incident of this kind must be reported."

She contacted the owner of the restaurant, logged his report into the records, and subsequently made a formal report to battalion headquarters.

It felt good to get back with my group for training on the searchlight. The responsibility of running a camp of almost fifty *inmates* reminded me of what my dad used to say: "To mind a group of highly spirited young women is much more difficult than to manage a bag full of fleas." How right he was.

One incident I simply ignored and never put into my report was the time when Trudi stepped out one night and stayed out for several hours. Only the girl in the bunk below and the two girls in the next bunk knew about it. They had an appropriate welcome prepared for Trudi's return around midnight. Because they had removed the wooden slats under the mattress in a certain way, she came tumbling down, mattress and all, as she climbed up into her bunk. The girl in the bottom bunk had moved out ahead of time, lying in ambush in another bunk. I pretended not to notice the reason for the commotion and requested that order be restored. *What I don't know, I don't have to report.*

Near the end of 1944, we busied ourselves closing up the camp for the projected move into individual batteries. We were told to take care of our personal property only. Everything needed from camp was transported by truck, while a second truck dropped predesignated groups of girls at their final destinations. All personnel turned to action with a feverish pitch, which made camp feel like a huge restless beehive, revolving around Queen Bee Miss Klein.

What would the next few weeks and months have in store for us? With the new year just around the corner, we all had the same fervent wish for the coming year: "Let this war come to an end soon so that we can return home."

* * *

Army Communiqué

December 16, 1944: German forces took the Allies by surprise as a sharp counterattack was launched in the Ardennes. It was hoped to reverse recent setbacks in Belgium and France.

December 29, 1944: The American expression "Nuts," as in "Nuts to you," has become the rallying cry for Allied troops besieged by Germans in the battle of Ardennes. "Nuts" was the defiant one-word reply from Brigadier General McAuliffe when the Germans demanded he surrender the city of Bastogne.

January 1, 1945: Hitler breaks his five-month silence to tell the German people that war will not end until the Reich is victorious.

*   *   *

7

Active Service on the Searchlight

Within the first few days of the new year, we moved to our new stations around the adjacent countryside. The batteries, the smallest unit in a regiment, had their entire compounds out in the flatland—dug in, with only the rooftops showing aboveground, for camouflage and security.

An average-size battery layout measured forty feet by forty feet and consisted of a two-room main building with a small annex in the back, plus an outdoor toilet. The sleeping quarters for the twelve of us girls measured ten feet to a side and had six double-stacked bunks. Our lockers took up most of the space against one wall. The second room of the same size, located toward the front of the building, became our living room, sparsely furnished with a table, several chairs, a bookcase, and very little extra space. The bookcase held our helmets, gas masks, and other military items. We felt like a bunch of sardines living in a can, but we managed.

I found it definitely bizarre for the washbasin, with its cold-water faucet, to be located in one corner of the living quarters, devoid of any partition whatsoever. We had to conduct our daily striptease and cleanup job in full view of anybody present. Since I felt very uncomfortable with that kind of an arrangement, I hurried through our morning ritual, while the eleven other girls milled about.

The niche of a kitchen protruded to one side of the living room. It held a two-burner cooktop, a small sink, wooden shelves for dishes, two large pots, one large fry pan, and an old barrel in the corner that substituted as a wastebasket.

The nook was in every way a very simple and compact, but workable kitchen.

The annex toward the back of the compound housed three elderly men in their sixties, drafted under the For Freedom and Life Act implemented in September 1939. They were to oversee the entire operation and assist us in case of emergency. Although our cook, one of the girls, prepared meals for the men also, none of us ever set foot into their strictly off-limits quarters. Their meals were delivered as far as their threshold and no further.

The searchlight itself was located to one side within the compound. A heavy removable metal shield protected it from the elements when not in use.

I will forever remember what I learned in training: The covering glass eye shield was 150 centimeters in diameter, with the same size concave glass *Parabol lens* behind it. Underneath the lens were carbon rods of different lengths—one 54-centimeter negative rod, one 84-centimeter positive rod, and one 16-centimenter ignition rod. The latter rod was sufficient for about seven hundred ignitions. After each engagement, the carbons had to be taken off and stored in a dry place. The covering eye shield needed careful removal by no less than four helpers in order to clean the *Parabol lens.* Only then could the eye shield be reinstalled.

A motor fed electricity to the ignition carbon rod, resulting in an arc of extremely bright light bridging between the negative and positive rods. Magnified by its huge lens, the searchlight's bright beam of light into the dark sky reached approximately thirteen miles vertically and up to seven miles horizontally.

At the beginning of the war, the most-used type of searchlights were the 150-centimeter *Flakscheinwerfer* 37. Searchlights were laid out in intervals of four kilometers between individual lights in a chessboard pattern. The searchlight zone, always located outside the FLAK engagement area, was the so-called "zone of preparation." Sound locators, and later fire-control radars, assisted the lights in finding their targets.

Crew in front of 200-centimeter searchlight

The more powerful 200-centimeter Flakscheinwerfer 40 entered service in 1942 and was usually positioned close to the radar of heavy *Flakbatteries,* which helped locate targets. When used in this fashion, the 200-centimeter light served as master light. As soon as the target was sighted, the three designated 150-centimeter satellite lights worked to trap the aircraft.

It was believed that a searchlight constituted an effective means of target defense in its own right. If one or more lights held a night bomber in their beams, the glare blinded its crew and possibly prevented any sort of accurate bombing run.

Next to the searchlight was the shed, which housed a twelve-cylinder Daimler-Benz motor, plus several large cylinders of bottled gas for fuel reserve. Only the larger and more modern 200-centimeter searchlights ran on regular gasoline, which of course was in short supply.

One large trench surrounded the entire area, guarded day and night by us draftees. Sentry duty required the guard, armed with a 98k army-issue rifle, to walk around the trench encircling the entire area. The appropriate password for entry to the compound was reported to us daily via field telephone from headquarters and had to be remembered by all of the crew.

One night, after my shift of guard duty ended and Mona took over, I handed her the rifle, as required.

"For heaven's sake, set the rifle down on the barrack wall," she said. "I'm afraid of that thing."

"But, Mona, we're required to carry it while on sentry duty."

"Yeah, I know. But it's loaded, and it scares me to death."

"Maybe you ought to take more instructions from one of the men on how to handle a loaded rifle, huh? I personally get a certain amount of comfort from the rifle when I'm out here all by myself for an hour, while all of you are asleep in there." I pointed to our quarters behind us.

During the night, one hour seemed like an eternity, alone in total darkness with only the stars overhead for company. While on duty, I slowly circled the entire compound several times. My head reached just above the trenches, looking out over a wide, flat, and frozen area covered with a few inches of snow. The snow-laden trees and bushes took on some odd shapes, like weird snow sculptures out of a fairy tale.

How long have I been out here? How soon will my relief sentry pop out of the front door? Pretty soon, I hope.

The extreme cold did not make guard duty any easier. Sometimes I hung around the recessed front door of our small barracks to find a bit of shelter from the howling winds. In spite of the earflaps on my wool cap pulled down all the way and my sentry overcoat with a lining of warm material clear down to my boots, the cold eventually reached my body, and I literally shivered in my boots.

I would panic at the slightest noise, like a dog barking or a tree branch breaking under a heavy load of snow. My mind immediately sprang to full attention, always anticipating a security check by the officer of the day. The hum of a car motor, followed by footsteps in the crunchy snow, indicated that someone from the military approached. Our post way out in the flatland had only a narrow dirt path leading to it, and townspeople had no reason to walk by.

Hey, engage your brain real quick, I told myself on one occasion when I heard footsteps. *What is the password for tonight?*

I grabbed the rifle and shouted, "Halt! Password!"

The sergeant major of the battalion was making a spot check. He gave the password.

"Permission granted to enter compound, Sergeant Major," I replied while standing at attention.

Sergeant Major Werner entered the compound and checked our quarters by standing at the threshold of the building without entering. He did a head count and then proceeded to the annex behind our dormitory to talk to the men.

I found out later that one of our girls had filed a complaint to the labor service leader about a Peeping Tom. One of the men in our battery was the suspect, and the sergeant major was investigating. Nothing more was heard about this case, but every one of the girls became doubly cautious.

I wanted very much to get out of dismal guard duty and therefore volunteered for cook's duty, mainly because the cook was released from standing guard at night and not because I loved to cook or knew a lot about cooking. However, as a cook, I had to get up one hour earlier than anybody else in order to prepare breakfast for twelve girls, plus the three men in the annex. Between breakfast in the morning, dinner at noon, coffee and a snack in the afternoon, and a cold supper at night, I had very little free time, while most of my comrades had a certain amount of leisure during the day. But I did get a few hours of uninterrupted sleep at night, provided there were no air raids. I still had the job of machinist, and when alerted by field telephone from FLAK battery, I had to be the first one to jump out of the bunk and get my coveralls on in seconds.

At this time of winter, it was pitch-dark by 6:00 p.m., and at this point we were on full alert; all of the crew had to be present at the station.

However, several times we had the unpleasant experience of an enemy fighter plane strafing the area around us in broad daylight.

"Alert, alert!" the sentry shouted. "Grab your helmets! Hit the trenches! Enemy airplane overhead!"

All of us dropped what we were doing, popped on our helmets, and jumped into the trenches. The antiaircraft guns of our nearest FLAK battery were already in action, and their rapid firing sounded like hundreds of thunderbolts during a wild summer rainstorm.

I saw the plane and heard the roaring of the motor as it soared in a fast, steep dive, guns blasting. Shrapnel hurtled downward with an eerie whistling sound that made my skin crawl. Crouched in the lowest point of the trench, I desperately wished for a hole to crawl into while holding my helmet with both hands. Suddenly, a bare four inches away from my head, a large piece of shrapnel buried itself into the dirt.

Wow, that was a close call. I shivered, and goose bumps rose on my arms.

After the danger passed, I dug out the large piece of shrapnel to keep as a souvenir. A quick survey showed no damage done by the strafing plane, and soon things went back to normal.

A short time later, we heard rumors through the grapevine about one of the neighboring stations. During a direct enemy attack, several of the girls became terribly frightened and ran for shelter away from their posts. An order issued by the regimental commander, a major, established that to leave the post under any circumstance was tantamount to desertion and cowardice before the enemy. Any soldier found guilty could and would be shot on the spot. *Lord help us all!*

The twelve of us knew our jobs and responsibilities. One volunteer was my helper on the Daimler-Benz motor. The seventeen-year-old took her job very seriously. However, at times, we both had trouble getting the motor started and would call one of the men in the annex for assistance. On one occasion, he pointed out that the lever on top of the gas bottle had been turned one notch too far, and the whole thing had frozen. No gas was released to the lines of the motor, and therefore the searchlight was rendered inoperable.

If any station did not light up immediately, an inquiry from battalion headquarters demanded an explanation.

The girls operating the searchlight were grouped in twos: one on the elevating lever for the vertical movement (zenith) and a backup. Another operated the searchlight's *Seitenrichtskala* for the horizontal movement (azimuth) with a backup helper. Another girl, wearing a headset, handled the field telephone directly connected with the FLAK battery commander, where in addition to the antiaircraft guns, they had sound locators, tracking telescopes, and numerous other technical equipment. The telephone operators at the various stations received the evaluation of the FLAK over the phone and relayed it to the girls operating the searchlight.

A total of sixteen individual searchlights in our battalion were required to light up in fours, meaning that four beams of light focused on one point: the enemy airplane.

Crew taking off cover to clean *Parabol* lens

It took willpower to do our job well. The threat of our top man, the major at the regimental level, always hung over us like Damocles's sword.

The night air raids continued around the city of Leipzig. Most of the time, the target was a very important plant manufacturing *Buna*, artificial rubber that had been developed during the ongoing war by German scientists and was of utmost importance to the war machine. No longer could rubber be imported from outside countries due to the almost total isolation of Germany.

During the raids on the *Buna-Werke* of Leipzig, everyone felt terror. The plant workers, however, kept on with their most important task: manufacturing tires for army trucks or air-force planes, plus many items needed for the navy. Nobody dared to give up, so work continued despite many odds. Eventually some of the manufacturing plants were shifted underground for security.

To everyone's surprise, several days without an air—raid or alert passed. One morning, during inspection of our station by the battalion lieutenant, he talked about a job opening at the *Schreibstube* (orderly room). A secretary, or as it was called there, *Schreiber*, was needed.

"Anybody interested and qualified, report to the battalion sergeant major," he said.

Immediately a bright light came on in my head.

Hey, that's the right job for me! It would get me out of this crummy double job of cook and machinist.

The very next morning, in full uniform, I requested to be excused from the compound in order to apply for the job at battalion headquarters. It was approximately a two-mile walk along the main road to the next village where the headquarters was located. I reported to Sergeant Major Werner, a tall, no-nonsense sort of a man. I applied for the job of *Schreiber*, stating my qualifications as a former secretary with good typing and shorthand capabilities. I took a brief test right then and there, and after a short wait, I was informed that I had the job.

Hurrah! I beat out the competition.

*　　*　　*

Army Communiqué

January 15, 1945: The Allied Forces' First Army entered the heart of Belgium, where some time later, the Battle of the Bulge was fought.

January 16, 1945: Prime Minister Winston Churchill of England warned Germany to surrender, stating that the Reich had less to fear from an unconditional surrender than from continuing a hopeless war.

*　　*　　*

8

THE ORDERLY ROOM

The next day, released from the searchlight station, I cleared out my locker, packed my trusty little cardboard suitcase with my meager belongings and my uniforms, and headed for my new job. I was elated over my advancement and full of hope and good intentions.

I took the same long country road as before to the next village until I reached the single-story, beige stucco building with a red-tiled roof—a former restaurant, and now battalion headquarters.

Several old signs advertising various brands of beer, lemonade, and other soft drinks—even a Coca-Cola sign—were still hanging on the wall next to the entrance. *What! Coca-Cola? That hasn't been available since the war started in September 1939.*

In front of battalion headquarters, the converted restaurant: Ruth, a young volunteer, and me

I found the side entrance of the orderly room, left my suitcase outside, walked in, and saluted the sergeant major. He introduced me to the second *Schreiber*, a seventeen-year-old volunteer who was to show me the premises.

The battalion commander, a first lieutenant, had a separate office next to the orderly room. The entire large basement, however, was occupied by the quartermaster, the *Feldzugmeister* and *Furier* for the battalion. The basement stored all kinds of food supplies and provisions as needed for the smooth operation of the searchlight battalion.

The restaurant's main room had been converted into the sick bay. Anneliese, a young draftee with basic knowledge in first aid, was in charge. A wooden screen separated her dormitory in one corner from the actual hospital room. The sick bay itself consisted of eight beds, several bedside tables, a large dining-room table, and six chairs. Everything looked clean, very simple, and rather plain, except for frilly white curtains on the windows, left over from the restaurant décor. A large, dark, old cabinet against one wall held the necessary medical supplies.

Ruth, a girl from our former camp, had started to work for the quartermaster a few days earlier and was at this time temporarily housed in the already overcrowded quarters nearby, a small barrack for military personnel.

She originally came from Gera, a medium-sized town twenty-five miles west of Leipzig. Ruth, blessed with an easygoing personality, was blonde, well built, and at least three inches taller than I was. In short order, we became good friends.

Because the army barracks nearby were already overcrowded, the sergeant major had to find permanent quarters in the private sector for Ruth and me. He gave us the address of the Schmitt family, and we were to contact them. All other details, he said, had been prearranged by headquarters.

"Just think, Ruth," I said. "We're going to live in private quarters in a small place of our own, away from the military crowd."

"I can hardly wait," she said, "because I'm crammed into the billets across the street, and there's absolutely no privacy for anybody. I hate it. Let's hope we'll get one room to ourselves with a decent bathroom instead of an outhouse."

Ruth and I, suitcases in hand, walked down the main road into the village, an eight-minute walk from headquarters. Off to the right of an alley stood a rather big two-story building. The large sign across the front of the house read, "Schmitt's Furniture Factory."

"I think we've arrived at our new home, Ruth. How do you like what you see?"

"Not too bad, so far."

Before entering the house, we quickly looked around. The courtyard located in front seemed large enough to park a couple of trucks. The side yard held various fruit trees, bare at this time of year. On the other side of the trees, a small hill sloped toward an unusual, tall, towerlike building outlining the sky. It reminded me of a Dutch windmill minus its blades.

"What do you think that is, Ruth?"

"Maybe a silo of sorts. After all, we're in farm country, remember?"

"How could I forget."

The furniture factory occupied the ground floor of the rectangular building, and the smell of fresh wood was noticeable everywhere. The second floor constituted the Schmitt family residence.

We contacted Mr. Schmitt at the downstairs factory, and he in turn introduced us to his daughter-in-law, who had been expecting us after being notified by Sergeant Major Werner. Young Mrs. Schmitt told us that she and her two children shared living quarters with her father-in-law, a widower. Her husband, Schmitt's son, had been in the army since the beginning of the war and at present time was somewhere on Russian soil.

Young Mrs. Schmitt, originally from Frankfurt, was delighted when she heard I hailed from the same area.

"I know Frankfurt endured many air raids. But is the Frankfurter Dom, that beautiful cathedral, still intact? How about the magnificent opera house on the *Opernplatz?* And what about the main station in the heart of Frankfurt?"

She asked question after question and felt distraught when I told her that bombs had destroyed the opera house, with only the facade remaining. Although she still had relatives around Frankfurt, she had not received any mail in a long time. She had heard only bits and pieces of news from the west via radio.

We had been walking upstairs while talking. Mrs. Schmitt showed us our quarters on the second floor. Next to our room was the family bathroom, which we would be allowed to share. We thanked her for her assistance and excused ourselves, as we were most anxious to inspect our new home.

We were ecstatic over what we found: The bedroom was very small, but tidy. It was barely big enough to hold two beds on opposite sides of the room, with a bedside table in-between. Wooden pegs fastened to the inside of the door could hold our clothes. Located next to the bedroom was the tiny corner of a kitchen consisting of a two-burner cooktop, a cabinet that served as pantry, and a small table with two chairs. Even the kitchen had a small window, covered with a simple white curtain, overlooking the courtyard.

What a wonderful difference from army quarters.

Ruth asked, "Which bed do you want, Ilsa? The one on the left or on the right?"

"Gosh! Ruth, I really don't care. I've never been asked which bunk I wanted. This is quite a heavy decision, huh? But since you give me a choice, I'll take the bed on the right. I prefer sleeping on my right side, and that way I can face the room with my back against the wall. Is that all right with you?"

"Fine with me." She smiled.

"Look at that," I repeated over and over. "All the comforts of home."

In no time at all, we felt right at home and enjoyed our free evenings away from the battalion, the sergeant major, and our comrades-at-arms. Ruth drew our daily rations directly from the quartermaster for whom she worked. After supper, we slipped into our pajamas and enjoyed the limited amount of freedom allowed us. We felt and talked like women without having to wear the uniform all the time or stand at attention if an officer were present.

Naturally, during our many evening conversations, the subject always turned to our families and sweethearts. Ruth had a boyfriend in the military, and she was very concerned about him.

"I have not had any mail from Richard for a long time," she said. "I'm really worried. He is somewhere in Russia, where all the heavy fighting is taking place. I wonder if his mother has heard from him in the meantime."

"Ruth, I know all too well how it feels not knowing about the one you love. The special man in my life is at present somewhere in Norway, and I have not had a letter from him for several months. We can only hope for the best, right?"

"Yeah, hope for the best—but be prepared for the worst. Isn't that the way it works?"

Ruth had requested a few days of emergency leave over the Easter holidays, which came up sometime in the middle of March.

"Can you believe that my younger brother has also been drafted since I left home?" she asked me. "Not only that, but my father, too, has been called to service under the For Freedom and Life Act. That leaves my mom completely alone to cope with these terrible times. And she is not healthy at all.

"I simply must get home for a few days to check on things," she continued. "It's only about twenty-two miles by train, and a couple of trains are still running. Wish me luck that I'll be granted a few days' leave of absence."

"You have all my good wishes, and I do hope you'll get to go home. Of course, I wish I could go home too—and never come back."

We talked for another few minutes before turning off the light, trying to fall sleep while all kinds of thoughts ran through our brains. The last thing I remembered before drifting off to dreamland was the wonderful smell of fresh-cut wood from the small mountain of shavings right under our bedroom window.

*　　*　　*

I liked the smell of freshly cut pine, oak, or even maple. It reminded me of the time back home as a young girl. I occasionally visited my oldest brother in his wood shop in Offenbach.

Fascinated with the various machines, the tools, the workbench, and the many different types of wood, I spun daydreams of what I could do with wood if I had the talent. During those visits, I often pretended to be a carpenter, picking up a plane to smooth a piece of rough wood or picking up a hammer and nails to work with scraps. Once I (almost) turned out a small sailboat—minus sails, of course. My left-handedness upset my brother. It looked awkward to him to see me swing a hammer and pound nails with my left hand.

"Just leave me alone, Otto. I'm doing all right with my left hand. You are just like Mama. When I try to slice a loaf of bread, she worries I could cut my throat instead."

*　　*　　*

The factory below our living quarters had many large, powerful, and noisy machines. Their unmistakable humming and clatter at times caused the floorboards of our studio apartment to vibrate. But after they shut down by nightfall, our evenings at home were pleasant and quiet, as were the weekends, when factories were closed.

We seldom saw our landlady. If we needed assistance with one thing or another, she always tried to be helpful. She even loaned us an old, plain little radio so that we could listen to the evening news or a few hours of music late at night. I found the foreign radio station of BBC London on our radio scale by accident. I recognized their radio signal by the very distinct sound of Big Ben chiming four times. I turned the sound somewhat louder, because, if possible, I wanted to find out how the war was *really* going.

"Verräter" (Traitor)

With great interest, I listened to their announcer; Peter Bergmann spoke excellent German and gave the British slant on the status of the war, although it most likely included a lot of propaganda from their side also—another reason all Germans were forbidden to tune in to foreign radio stations. If caught, they were branded traitors.

*   *   *

Army Communiqué

January 30, 1945: US troops have launched a drive on the Siegfried Line, a line of fortification along the border of France and Germany.

January 31, 1945: Soviet troops, in a blinding blizzard, are breaking through outer ring of Berlin in the East. German forces are pushed out of Russia and are retreating before the Soviet offensive.

February 3, 1945: Allied bombers have dropped 3,000 tons of bombs on Berlin.[2]

*   *   *

I liked my work in the orderly room, although it was very military in every way—almost like a nine-to-five job pressed into a uniform. With military punctuality, I was expected to arrive at work and always keep up with the workload. What I hated, though, was to have to stand at attention and offer the nationalistic salute every time an officer entered the room. The rest of my work I found relatively easy. I answered the field telephone, typed messages, or carried messages to military personnel within the battalion. The major bulk of my work was typing orders, distributing information throughout the battalion, and taking dictation for special letters to the command center, plus a few odd jobs sprinkled in between.

---

[2] When it happened, we heard bits and pieces about this horrific, deadly air raid via radio and through conversations with people around us. However, we did not initially realize the full extent of the terror and misery caused by such a raid. If one bomb could bring death, what possible damage could 3,000 tons do?

The first lieutenant in charge was in every way a stickler for proper German. His dictation was precise and to the point, but he argued with the spelling and punctuation of every letter that came across his desk for signature. At first it annoyed me—to say the least. But as I became more familiar with the military style of writing and gathered more confidence in myself along the way, I started arguing with him—in a cautious sort of way, of course.

"What makes you think you are right and I am wrong?" he asked at one point.

"Because, Lieutenant, before the war, I took special language classes in German after receiving my diploma in business administration. My goal was to become an efficient secretary, and the emphasis in this particular class was proper German, both verbal and written. If I may say so myself, I know my German pretty well, and the instructor of the class, a professor of the German language, must have thought so, too, because I received a good grade in the finals."

The lieutenant looked curiously at me as if suddenly seeing me for the very first time. When I turned completely around to get a good look at him, a realization dawned:

Hmm, he's kind of handsome. Maybe midthirties. His stocky build and broad shoulders cut a handsome figure in his Luftwaffe uniform. With his blond hair and blue eyes, he would qualify for the epitome of the pure-bred Aryan, as often shown on propaganda posters of the National Socialist Party.

*   *   *

Army Communiqué

February 11, 1945: The Big Three (Churchill, Roosevelt, and Stalin) are holding their famous meeting in Yalta.

At that meeting, The Big Three will have to smooth the feathers of those who felt they had been arbitrarily excluded from Yalta.

General de Gaulle of France is particularly upset.

On the same date: 1,200 RAF planes have blasted Wiesbaden and Karlsruhe.

February 13 and 14, 1945: Allied and British planes have devastated Dresden in a two-day raid. The city was considered Germany's gem, called "the Florence of Germany." Priceless art and architecture from the seventeenth and eighteenth centuries have been destroyed.[3]

*   *   *

One week later, the sergeant major requested that I immediately finish a rather lengthy, but important, letter to the regimental commander, and to have it signed by the lieutenant and sent out via battalion motorcycle courier the same evening.

However, by the time I had completed the letter, the lieutenant had already left for his quarters, a prefabricated wooden building in close proximity to headquarters and next door to a searchlight battery.

I put on my uniform jacket, buttoned it up, and popped on the ugly hat, and off I went to the lieutenant's quarters, letter in hand. (Men's quarters were strictly off-limits to all females.)

At least ten pairs of eyes from the searchlight crew next door looked me over with curiosity and suspicion as I walked past their station to the front door of the lieutenant's quarters. Most of the girls knew me by sight and knew I worked in the orderly room, but they remained suspicious nevertheless,

---

3   Reports state that approximately 130,000 people were killed. The exact death toll could never be established. At the time of the raid, Dresden had given shelter to tens of thousands of unregistered refugees and expellees from the eastern part of Germany, as well as from parts of Poland and Russia.

because I was headed for the lieutenant's quarters. I felt uncomfortable under their scrutiny.

I waved my hand in a short and friendly greeting and held the large yellow envelope in plain sight. *Oh, these women. I'd better watch my step.*

I knocked on the lieutenant's door. He opened the door after the third knock and seemed surprised to see me standing there in full uniform.

"Lieutenant Schröder, this letter"—I held up the envelope—"requires your signature. Sergeant Major Werner stated it was urgent, and it is to go out by courier this evening."

"Do come in and sit here while I read the letter."

He pointed toward a plain sofa placed against the wall of the front room.

I quickly took my ugly hat off, making sure my hair was in place, and sat down, glancing around the room. It was clean but sparsely furnished, not unlike our own quarters at the various batteries. Just the utmost necessities—nothing fancy or pretty. A framed picture of a woman sat on the bookshelf. *I wonder if that's his wife.* I knew the lieutenant was married, just like the sergeant major and some of the other sergeants at headquarters. All of the female draftees, however, were single. (Married women, and especially those with children, were exempt from the draft.)

Lieutenant Schröder sat at his desk, concentrating on the letter. He was in shirtsleeves, but still wore his boots.

Hmmm, yes, he looks nice. One of the nicest-looking men I've seen in a long time.

My nerves tingled as I sat staring at his back, nervously crumpling my hat between my hands.

If only he would sign the letter quickly, so I can get out of here before I say or do something absolutely stupid.

Seconds seemed to turn into hours, but finally he signed and sealed the letter.

The lieutenant rose and turned to me.

I nervously stood up to face him.

"My compliments. You did a good job on this letter," he said with a faint smile.

I was happy about his compliment, yet nervous. I felt strangely uncomfortable to stand so close to this handsome man.

"Thank you, Lieutenant," I replied.

Before handing me the letter, he put both hands on my shoulder.

"Your first name is Ilsa, right?"

"Yes." I nodded.

He continued talking while his hands rested on my shoulders.

"You are from the Frankfurt area? Well, I am from Würzburg, and that is where my family lives. Mail is slow in coming through, and I have not received any mail for weeks."

"Yes, Lieutenant, I know. I, too, am very unhappy about that. I have not heard from my family in quite a while. I'm very concerned about their well-being, with the air raids and all—" My voice trailed off in an unfinished sentence.

Lieutenant Schröder pulled me closer to him in a tight hug.

"Yeah, this terrible war," he said in a very low voice. "When will it ever come to an end? We all have suffered over the years. No one can escape its misery."

I looked at him with curious surprise, because I knew the danger of making these kinds of statements, particularly by an officer of the Luftwaffe. *Does this mean he trusts me?* A reassuring, warm feeling came over me, and with a happy smile, I lifted my face and inched a bit closer to him.

What followed was a bear hug, followed by a tender kiss. For a few split seconds, I forgot my problems, my heartache, and even this terrible war.

How heavenly to be in the embrace of a man—a handsome and intelligent man at that. Put your head on his shoulder, Ilsa. Try to forget this rotten world for a few minutes. Savor this moment, come what may.

But rather suddenly, a major alarm went off in my head:

Remember where you are and who you are with! Did you forget the ten pairs of eyes right outside the door, ten nosy minds probably counting the minutes until your reappearance outside? You need to get yourself out of the lieutenant's quarters as fast as you can, or else you'll be in deep trouble—and the lieutenant, too!

"Sorry," I said softly and abruptly pulled away.

I turned, grabbed the letter and my hat, smoothed down my hair, checked my uniform, and headed for the door. At the threshold, I saluted, closed the door, and turned the corner of the building in a big hurry, my mind still in a whirl. *What if . . .*

In big strides, I rushed back to the office to catch the courier and handed him the letter. For a moment, I stood watching as the young corporal kicked down the starter on the heavy motorcycle, revved the motor, put it into gear, and rode off into the sunset.

Just like in a movie. Yeah, maybe a war movie.

Slowly I made my way home to my quarters at the Schmitt Factory. I needed a little time to think before I met Ruth at the apartment.

I made up my mind:

Don't tell. What an upsetting but wonderful day, but you should never mention it to her or anybody else.

Work at the orderly room went on as usual. My superior, the sergeant major, treated me well. He demanded a lot in terms of work performance, but I could handle that. The lieutenant held our interactions to a business-only standard, yet he maintained a courteous, almost respectful manner toward me. Secretly I felt a certain amount of admiration for him. For a few seconds during our short encounter, I had seen beyond the dedicated officer in uniform and gotten a glimpse of a warm, compassionate human being seemingly troubled by a relentless and escalating war.

One change I noticed in the office: more frequently, the male staff members talked seriously, but in low voices, among themselves. I figured this was because of the escalation of the war. BBC London reported that the American forces had already infiltrated German soil, while public reports from the German War Department were vague and fuzzy. To really grasp the total picture and to understand where this war machine was headed was impossible.

My frustration increased, multiplied by a feeling of helplessness. My worries about my family back home also wore me down. If the war escalated on all fronts, it seemed clear to me that the bombing raids on the entire country would increase as well.

*   *   *

Army Communiqué

February 28, 1945: US tanks have broken through the natural defense line west of the Rhine River and have crossed the Erft River.

March 2, 1945: Cologne (Köln) has fallen to General Hodges's First US Army. The army had to cross the Rhine River on the Ludendorff bridge at Remagen, between Cologne and Koblenz, before it could be destroyed by German forces. General Patton's tanks crossed on a pontoon bridge built within forty-eight hours by US Army engineers.

*   *   *

9

TROUBLE IS BREWING

The Easter holidays approached in the middle of March. Ruth received four days' emergency leave during Easter to visit her mother in Gera. She packed a few of her personal things into a bag to walk the two miles to the train station.

"Have a good trip, Ruth. I hope you find your mother well, and please give her my best wishes for a happy Easter."

"Thanks, I'll tell her. I doubt it could possibly be a happy Easter. We'll see. You take care of yourself, Ilsa. See you within four days. Good-bye."

Ruth left for the station, and I walked in the opposite direction to the office.

The two days of the Easter holiday passed; for many of us, it meant just another Sunday followed by a Monday. The relentless air raids didn't take a holiday; work went on all around me, with no days off for FLAK or searchlight crews, as enemy bombers flew their missions day and night. Amid destruction and loss of life in one part of the country or the other, the entire country was in a chokehold, gasping for life and struggling from day to day for survival.

My spirit was at an all-time low, and I felt the need to talk to somebody. After writing a letter to my boyfriend in Norway and one to my family in Offenbach, I decided to take a walk. It was a clear, cool day, and I headed uptown to visit Anneliese in sick bay. At present, she had two girls with minor illnesses from neighboring searchlight batteries in her ward. Most of the crew knew each other by sight from occasional battalion assemblies in the field, and many knew I worked in the orderly room.

"*Guten Tag*, Anneliese. How are you? Are you busy, or can I stay for a few minutes?" I waited for her reply at the threshold, holding the door open.

"Come in, Ilsa. I'm not busy right now. At the moment, we're taking a coffee break. Come join us. You want a cup of our *famous* brew?"

"Gee, thanks, Anneliese." I turned to her patients. "May I join you? It would be nice to have company for a change. Do you mind?"

"No, not at all," answered Käthi, who had her leg in a semicast. "Look at me, I sprained my left ankle so badly, I can hardly get around. But it's getting better. At least now I can stand."

"What happened?"

"Pure stupidity," she replied. "I jumped into the trench during an exercise, something I have done a hundred times. My foot turned sideways when I hit the ground. Boy, did that hurt."

"I think it's a hairline fracture," Anneliese interjected. "But we can't get it X-rayed; we don't have the necessary equipment here at battalion. I believe I straightened the ankle, and it will have to heal the way I set it."

The third girl looked at me with curiosity. "You work in the orderly room, right? Don't you live with a farm family somewhere in the village?"

"Yes, Ruth from the quartermaster and I live in a small one-room apartment on the second floor over the Schmitt Furniture Factory. It's right down the road, about eight minutes from here."

The nurse introduced the girl to me as Lotte; Lotte was from a searchlight battery in a nearby village. Admitted to sick bay several days earlier with painful cramps in her lower abdomen, she was now on the mend.

"I met Ruth," Lotte said. "While drawing rations for my team from the quartermaster, I had the chance to speak to her a few times. I'm curious—where is she today?"

"Well, lucky Ruth got a four-day pass to go home to Gera and visit her mother over the Easter holiday. It was somewhat of an emergency. She should be back here within a couple of days."

"Darn, I didn't know we could get a pass to go home," Lotte said.

"I think it's because the majority of girls come from greater distances, and can't go home and make it all the way back in four days."

Lotte gave a deep sigh. "What I wouldn't give to go home and see my folks. Can you believe I was kind of happy when I got the draft notice last October? I wanted to get away from home in the worst possible way. My folks have a small farm in an out-of-the-way place near Eppertshausen, in the Rodgau District. I always hated farm life. But compared to this"—she made a sweeping gesture with her hand—"it would now seem like paradise."

"Touché," we all said in unison.

All of us evidently had the same thought at this moment: we wanted to go home. The conversation turned to what we would do, if only . . . If only we knew the truth about the war. If only the mail would come through, and we heard from our families. If only the war would end. *If, if, if. What a small word.*

After about twenty minutes, I decided to go back to my quarters. I thanked Anneliese for the coffee and bid everyone good-bye. Anneliese walked with me to the door, and we stepped outside.

"I must tell you something I did not want the other girls to hear." She lowered her voice to a whisper. "Do you know the shoemaker in town? I believe his name is Rasch, or Rausch, or something similar."

"No." I shook my head, puzzled. "Why?"

"Rumor has it, the shoemaker is a member of the Jehovah's Witnesses. They're blacklisted by the party, as you probably know. Local leaders had him arrested once or twice for his anti-nationalistic political views. The government watches this church and its members closely. The shoemaker has been in trouble before for his belief, but he seems well informed about political matters and allegedly knows about the status of the war. If only we could talk to him. This not-knowing and the uncertainty of it all drives me up a wall."

"Thanks for confiding in me, Anneliese. Who knows? This information might come in handy one of these days. I'll keep it strictly to myself. You are so right. If only someone would tell us the truth so that we knew where we stood, right? Well, we just have to wait and see. Take care of yourself and your patients. I'll be seeing you again soon. *Auf Wiedersehen!*"

She bid me good-bye, and I walked slowly back along the main road to my quarters. Desperately trying to shake my down-in-the-dumps feeling, I decided to spruce up the apartment before Ruth returned.

Like a busy little housewife, I cleaned the tiny kitchen and our small bedroom, dusted our sparse furniture, and wiped the windows. I sorted my clothes and washed undergarments and other small items, hanging everything neatly on a makeshift drying line in the kitchen. Finally, I washed up for the night and rolled my hair in wooden rollers held with elastic bands. The clock read 11:00 p.m.

High time to go to bed. Tomorrow is another day. Maybe things will look a bit better. Darn these wooden rollers! It's uncomfortable to sleep with these in my hair.

The next morning, I went to work at the battalion. When I came home to our quarters early that evening, Ruth had already returned from Gera. I sensed immediately something terribly wrong. Upset and on the verge of tears, she gave me a welcome hug.

"What's the matter, Ruth? What happened?"

"Oh, Ilsa, it was awful! When I got to Gera, I had to walk all the way to my home from the train station, because no public transportation was available. The town had been bombed the night before and was horribly damaged. As I turned into our street and approached our house, I found only the facade and the bare chimney still standing in a heap of rubble."

"My God, Ruth, is your mom all right?"

"Yes, more or less. I frantically searched for her, and with the help of a neighbor, I found her in the basement of our house. She was all right, but very upset and disoriented. Lucky for us, Dad had converted the basement into an air-raid shelter before his call to service. The basement had been reinforced with heavy beams, and even an old bed sat in the corner. After the raid, one of the neighbors checked on Mom off and on, but everybody in the neighborhood had their own problems. Many people were in a similar situation as my mother, but some lost family members in the raid. It was just awful."

"Ruth, why didn't you stay home with your mom, where you're really needed? Why come back here? What for, really?"

"Well, I'm going back as soon as I can get my things together. I wanted to pick up my clothes and other items. A lot was destroyed in the house, and what I left behind here is more important now than ever. I'm going to pack it all up and catch the next train back."

"I'm truly sorry. Let me help you. I'll walk with you to the train station. Do you have a return ticket?"

"Yes, I bought it at the station upon my arrival. The next train leaves in two hours. It is 6:00 p.m. now—that'll give me one and a half hours to get ready. It's about a thirty-five-minute walk to the station."

We packed as much into her small suitcase as it would hold. The remainder, like shoes, pictures, and an old raincoat, I wrapped into a medium cardboard box that I tied with heavy string, fashioning the ends of the string into a handle to make carrying easier. As we left the house, we ran into our landlady.

"Hello, ladies. Where are you going in such a hurry?" she asked.

"To catch a train," Ruth answered as we hurried away.

Ruth and I talked about the danger of leaving the unit without permission during wartime. I was not too worried about myself, since I would return to my quarters and go to work the next morning, as usual.

"They'll have to catch me first!" was Ruth's final comment.

The route to the station brought us in close proximity to one of the outlying searchlight batteries. Some of the crew milled about inside the compound and spotted us.

"Hey, where are you going?" they called.

Ruth and I were in uniform, and the girls knew we belonged to their battalion.

"For a walk," we shouted and waved back.

They're probably wondering why we're carrying a suitcase and a box on a string. Well, let them wonder. It's none of their business.

The train station was not too crowded. The train rolled in; a few passengers got off, and a few more boarded. I bade a sad good-bye to Ruth, knowing full well we would probably never see each other again. She boarded the train.

"Ilsa, take care of yourself. Keep your chin up! So long!"

The train rolled out.

"Good luck, Ruth!" I shouted.

In another minute, the train passed out of sight. Heavyhearted, I walked back to town and felt ill at ease as my inner voice repeated, *I hope they don't catch her. I hope they don't catch her.*

10

Under House Arrest

A knock on my door came the minute I had returned to my quarters. Somehow my sixth sense registered imminent trouble waiting outside, and I was right.

The top labor service leader, Miss Gehrig, stood at the threshold with an unmistakably stern expression on her face.

My pulse beat strongly in my throat, and I felt as if my knees would buckle. *How the heck did she get here so quickly? And who notified her in the first place?* My mind raced over the earlier events of the day. *Did the girls from the outlying searchlight battery notify headquarters? I'll bet the landlady contacted our leader.*

I desperately tried to pull myself together and remain calm.

"Do come in, Miss Gehrig." I stepped back from the open door.

"Where have you been, and where is Ruth?" Her voice was harsh and cold.

Before I could answer, I swallowed hard.

"Ruth has gone back to Gera to be with her mother."

"What do you mean, she has gone back to be with her mother?" Miss Gehrig demanded.

"Ruth was terribly upset over the fact that her mother suffered a nervous breakdown after the last air raid. She found her mother in a state of shock in the basement of their bombed-out home. There wasn't anybody left to care for her. Ruth felt it necessary to return home."

Miss Gehrig gave me an angry look, her right index finger pointing accusingly.

"Do you realize what the two of you have done? You cannot just walk away from your assigned post in a time of war! Nor can you help anybody to walk away from an oath to serve the Fatherland. Ruth will be charged with desertion, and you with assistance to desertion. There will be the necessary investigation and a court-martial to follow."

My heart skipped a beat. I leaned against the nearest wall so as not to faint. My mind whirled. *This is serious. Why didn't I get away, too? Why did I walk with Ruth to the train station? Maybe I should have pretended I was asleep while Ruth packed. No, nobody would have believed that version. What will the regimental commander say? Furthermore, what will he do?*

A cold sweat came over me, and my thoughts turned toward my mother, sister, and niece. *Will I ever see them again? Will I be incarcerated for assistance to desertion . . . or even worse?*

My whole body trembled with fear, yet through a fog, I heard Miss Gehrig say, "Pack a few necessities together. You will be under house arrest and confined to the battalion sick bay, where you will remain until further notice."

I pulled my suitcase out from its hiding place underneath my bed and threw a few personal things into it. My hands shook so badly that I kept knocking things off the bedside table. I felt faint and terribly scared at the same time. *What will happen to me now?* The big lump in my throat took my breath away. I felt a sharp pain in the pit of my stomach. *Now what?*

Old Eagle Eyes watched my every move. As soon as I closed my suitcase, she ushered me out of the room.

We walked in silence along the main road to battalion headquarters, which seemed miles away. Sergeant Major Werner and his staff sergeant met us in front of the building. They were in the process of mounting one of the big military motorcycles with an attached sidecar. From the conversation between Miss Gehrig and the sergeant major, I gathered they were headed toward Gera to catch up with the train and arrest Ruth. As he kicked down the starter of the cycle, the sergeant major turned briefly to me without addressing me by name.

"If we catch Ruth, you will get off lightly," he said. "But if we don't, the charge of assistance to desertion still stands."

I felt crushed, and my feelings vacillated like a teeter-totter. *I hope they don't catch Ruth . . . but on the other hand, what will happen to me if they don't?*

With teeth clenched, I turned around and walked toward the main door to the sick bay, where I met Anneliese. She saluted Miss Gehrig and received instructions from her concerning my house arrest. Under no circumstances was I to leave sick bay, and Anneliese was responsible for keeping an eye on me. Our leader left.

By order of Miss Gehrig, my uniform was taken away from me and put in safekeeping. I had to wear the simple blue short-sleeved work dress. Since it was still pretty cold at the end of March, I was allowed to wear a sweater. Anneliese gave me a choice of bed. I emptied my suitcase, put the rest of my things into the locker on the wall, and set two small family pictures on the bedside table. I made sure I kept my distance from everybody, thinking it best for all concerned.

I gave my sincere promise to Anneliese to not do anything foolish, like running away or anything else that was stupid. I felt she understood my feelings and trusted me in spite of the uproar all of this had caused.

The next day, I was ordered into a small room next to sick bay. Miss Gehrig and our leader from camp, Miss Klein, were present to interrogate me as to the why and how.

Miss Gehrig opened the interrogation.

"Ruth could not be apprehended; the sergeant major returned with an empty sidecar. Before we go any further, I must ask you for a detailed account of what happened between the two of you prior to Ruth's desertion."

I had to swallow hard to keep my feelings in check, yet I was glad Ruth had not been apprehended.

"Miss Gehrig, as I told you, when Ruth came back, she was very upset, because there had been a terrible air raid in Gera, and her mother had suffered a nervous breakdown."

"But what made her decide to leave her designated post and go back home to Gera?" Miss Klein interjected.

"Ruth felt she had to take care of her mother after finding her amid a heap of rubble on a cot in what was left of the basement. She was disoriented, alone, and helpless. There wasn't anybody in the neighborhood who could care for her; everybody had problems of their own. Many houses were bombed out, with the water and gas mains broken and electricity shut off. Some of her friends and neighbors had been killed or were badly injured. Ruth felt as if she had to stay and take care of her mother."

"But Ruth came back here to her quarters. What was that all about?" Miss Klein asked.

"Yes, she came back for the few belongings she had left here. After all, she lost almost everything in Gera. She could not afford to lose any more."

"You were an accomplice to her desertion. What were you thinking of when you assisted her in her plans to desert her unit?" Miss Gehrig demanded, giving me a very cold and stern stare.

"I did not see it in those terms," I replied. "I saw my friend in distress. I wanted to help, and that was the only thought I had. I helped her pack, and I walked with her to the train station."

"Well," Miss Klein said, "I am very much surprised about your attitude in this matter. I always thought of you as a patriotic, sincere, and righteous member of our outfit. Why else would I have appointed you to run the camp in Pölzig during my absence? I had a lot of confidence in your sincerity and your ability to serve your Fatherland. Only now does it become apparent that I was sadly mistaken.

"It was also reported that you frequently listened to foreign stations on your radio. I'm convinced you know that such things are absolutely verboten under penalty of law. What on earth were you thinking?"

"Sorry if I disappoint you, Miss Klein, but I cannot change the way I feel and have been feeling for years about all of this—the service, the hardship connected with it, the frustration in particular, and the war in general. When will it all come to an end?"

I was fully aware that I was in dangerous territory, the way I talked, and the painful knot returned to my stomach. But with my back pushed against an invisible wall, I felt I had not much more to lose. A court-martial was imminent, and the mere thought of it scared the hell out of me. My mind conjured up a picture of the top man in our battalion, the major, making mincemeat out of me.

I received a long patriotic sermon from both leaders with an admonition not to cause any trouble whatsoever—to keep myself available and above all, to not try anything stupid like running away, as Ruth had done. The latter thought had crossed my mind many times, but by now it was too late to even try, because several parties were watching me closely. Besides, I had no money or regular street clothes, and without either one, I could not get very far. I decided to put my faith and hope in the American troops advancing from the west; their timely arrival might put an end to all of my worries.

The days that followed seemed to crawl at a snail's pace. I felt isolated and depressed. My little world had been compressed to one corner of the sick bay: a bed, a bedside table, and a chair. Absolutely no news trickled down to me, whether good or bad. There wasn't anybody I could talk to. However, Anneliese at times would say a few encouraging words to me, provided we were alone.

"Don't worry too much, Ilsa. All is not lost. You wait and see!"

"Please, Anneliese, I must ask you for a big favor: I would like to take a pair of shoes to the shoemaker. They badly need to be repaired. If I promise not to do anything foolish, will you allow me to go across the street for just a few minutes? I'll only drop off my shoes and come right back. They are my uniform shoes. The only other pair I have are my old loafers I brought from home."

"Sure." Anneliese nodded. "Go ahead. I trust you. But please hurry, because you are not to leave here at all, remember?"

"Oh, I know," I replied with a faint shrug of my shoulders. "I have never felt so helpless in all my life. But then, I have never been incarcerated before, either."

We exchanged an understanding glance, and I felt she knew the real reason I wanted to see the shoemaker. Without more conversation, I grabbed my shoes and headed across the street.

On the ground floor of his modest house, the middle-aged man with grayish hair, Mr. Rasch, worked in a room amid a clutter of shoes, bags, and even old suitcases. With a cobbler's anvil between his knees, he nailed a new heel on an old boot that, from the looks of it, had seen better days. But everything was in short supply, especially shoes, and therefore repairs were made over and over until the item finally fell apart. The room had a smell of leather, glue, shoe dye, and polish.

"Good morning," I said.

Mr. Rasch turned around, hammer in hand, looking at me through glasses that had slipped down his nose a bit.

"Good morning. What can I do for you?" He spotted the pair of shoes in my hand. "Let me see those shoes. Hmm, army shoes."

"Yes, Mr. Rasch, I'm a drafted member of the searchlight battalion across the street." To gain his confidence, I added, "At present time under house arrest at battalion sick bay."

After giving my name and my hometown, I gave him a very short account of what had happened.

"I know, Mr. Rasch, you cannot say very much. I know you have been in trouble with the local authorities over political matters. But, please, listen to my plea, because I am very scared of what else can or will happen to me. I just don't know what to do. Do you have any advice?"

"Go back to the sick bay," he said in a very calm voice. "Don't worry. It will all be over soon. The American troops are very close. Come back tomorrow to pick up your shoes; you certainly will need them if and when you go home. And now, you better hurry back. *Auf Wiedersehen.*"

"*Auf Wiedersehen*, Mr. Rasch, and thank you very much for talking to me. I feel so much better already. I'll see you tomorrow."

I hurried back on feet that felt as if they had been given wings. I owed Anneliese consideration and did not want her to get into trouble by allowing me to leave, even if only for a few minutes. I practically flew across the street to the sick bay. Anneliese greeted me with a most curious look.

"Is everything all right? You certainly look happier. Good news?"

"Yes, Anneliese, good news, but we'll discuss it later—I hope you understand. My shoes will be ready tomorrow. Do you think I can go to pick them up in the afternoon?"

"I think so. I will make my daily report by field telephone around noontime. By then I should know if anyone from the leadership might stop by. It probably will be safe for you to go. We'll see."

For the rest of the afternoon, I stayed in my designated little corner of the sick bay. Around 6:30 p.m., I quietly ate my supper, cold cuts and a kind of herbal tea, after which I retreated back to my corner. My mind, cluttered with thousands of thoughts, kept searching for various alternatives and solutions to my predicament.

At noon the following day, I got the go-ahead to retrieve my shoes. To my surprise, Mr. Rasch did not charge me at all for the minor repair.

"I'm glad I could be of help," he said and handed me my shoes. "Do not worry too much about your predicament. Help is on the way. Keep your mouth shut and just wait."

I thanked him and made a quick exit. I took the outer stone steps of battalion headquarters in one big jump and pushed the big wooden door open, almost colliding with a young comrade-at-arms who evidently had just seen Anneliese, judging from her bandaged forearm.

"Excuse me," I said. "I'm sorry—guess I should slow down, huh?"

Anneliese was busy by the medicine cabinet, sorting a supply of bandages and ointments. She gave me an inquisitive look. "Are you all right?"

Holding the shoes over my head, I danced to the tune of an imaginary waltz, turning and bouncing until I reached my bed and plopped down on it.

"Does that answer your question?" I quipped.

"You must be crazy." She shook her head. "See you in a little while."

I nodded and put the shoes into my locker.

A few hours later, I had a chance to catch her alone. I told her about the possibility of a big change in the making and rumors that the American troops were very close.

"Oooh!" she said with raised eyebrows.

I put my index finger over my mouth to indicate that we must keep our mouths shut.

Anneliese winked.

That particular night, I slept a lot better. I could finally hope again.

The days went by, and with each passing day, the muffled sound of heavy artillery fire at a distance grew louder. I often sat by the window, facing the street, and with great curiosity watched the increased activity all around. I noticed a restlessness among the battalion staff, a coming and going all day long as if somebody or something stirred up an anthill. *There's definitely something ominous in the air.*

* * *

Army Communiqué

April 1, 1945: Paris has lit the Arc de Triomphe and Cathédrale Notre Dame for the first time since the start of war.

April 10, 1945: British Eighth Army tanks have launched a major offensive in Italy.

*   *   *

11

SUDDEN CHANGE OF EVENTS

In the early morning of April 11, all hell broke loose. (Incidentally, it happened to be my birthday.)

A short message from our top labor service leader came over the field telephone to all units. It was the official, verbal release from our oath to the Fatherland.

Wow—what is happening? Is this the end of the war? Does this mean our freedom from service? What are we going to do now?

The leader's message suggested strongly that we vacate all military premises as soon as possible, draw final rations from the quartermaster and collect our money (monthly soldier's pay) from the finance agent. Finally, we were told, "then you may go wherever you want to go."

This last statement stunned me.

Where do I want to go? Home, of course!

The latest news was that the Russian forces were advancing from the east, while the American troops marched in from the west.

Well, since my home was in the west, I would have to take my chances and eventually pass through the territory held by American troops. Under no circumstances did I want to face Russian troops, remembering the many terrible stories my two brothers had told me concerning their war experiences on Russian soil.

Wow! What a wonderful present, to be released on my birthday. First of all, it meant my freedom from incarceration, and more importantly, my freedom from court-martial.

I jumped for joy, and within minutes and with great speed, I packed my meager belongings into my cardboard suitcase.

At this point in time, I had only one prevalent thought: *Get the heck out of here as fast as possible.*

I was still wearing the blue work dress, so I retrieved my uniform, changed, and within minutes was ready to leave.

"So long, Anneliese. I'm going back to my quarters at the Schmitt family. I'm very curious just what Mrs. Schmitt will have to say to me or how she might act toward me in view of what has happened. I still have some of my belongings there. Besides, I have no other place to bunk down and she owes me some consideration. We'll see.

"Anneliese, please put out the word: we must meet here at sickbay as soon as possible so that we all can discuss our plans for our return home."

"I sure will. Gosh, if I only knew what to do now. Here we are, 320 miles from home and no transportation whatsoever, not even a bicycle."

"I know what you mean. It's going to be a long walk."

We were all in a tizzy. Some of Anneliese's patients also left shortly to return to their stations, if for no other reason but to touch base with their comrades and retrieve their belongings. Anneliese and another girl stayed behind.

"Let's all meet here tomorrow morning," Anneliese said to every girl as they headed out the door. "We are now more or less on our own and have to make plans accordingly. We must rely on each other and make plans for our return home."

"Good suggestion. Everyone knows how to get to sick bay. We'll spread the word."

When I reached the Schmitt Factory, I rang young Mrs. Schmitt's apartment. She seemed surprised to see me again so soon. I told her of the battalion order to vacate all military premises and therefore was hoping that I could have my old room back for a few days until I figure out what to do next. With almost uncanny politeness toward me, she handed me the key to my quarters. Our conversation was rather short and somewhat awkward. I thanked her for the key and said good-bye as I closed the door behind me. With a big sigh of relief I finally sat down on my bed.

I slept kind of restlessly that night; the artillery fire grew louder, and it seemed at times very close.

*   *   *

Army Communiqué

April 12, 1945: Franklin D. Roosevelt has died on the eve of victory. The unexpected death of the thirty-first president of the United States stunned the nation and the world. The White House flag is lowered to half-staff, marking the death of an occupant.

Harry S. Truman assumed the presidency just hours after the death of FDR. Truman now has the job of ending the war.

April 15, 1945: The USSR honored Franklin D. Roosevelt by flying black-bordered flags on government offices.

*   *   *

The next morning, I dressed in a hurry to walk to battalion headquarters, which at this point was still operating full force. I could draw my last *Sold* (soldier's pay) and last ration, along with ration tickets good for fresh bread, luncheon meat, one pound of sugar, and a half a pound of salt. It wasn't much, and I knew I must be very careful with my rations, not knowing where the next meal would come from.

I also stopped at sick bay to say hello to Anneliese and a few of the girls who had arrived ahead of me. Hilde, from my hometown of Offenbach, stood by one of the windows with a forlorn expression, watching the stir below. When she spotted me, she walked over.

"Hello," she said. "I heard the girls were meeting here this morning, so I came over from my battery to see what's going on. All my belongings are still over there, because I don't really know what to do next. I have no place in particular I could go to. What are you going to do, Ilsa?"

"Well, I was kind of lucky, I guess. I returned last night to my quarters with the Schmitt family in town, and I hope to stay there in spite of the trouble I had in the past with young Mrs. Schmitt, until I see my way clear to start for home." I paused for a few seconds.

"You know what, Hilde? I have a great idea. Will you walk back with me to see Mrs. Schmitt? I feel she owes me for the problems she had caused. Maybe she'll agree that you could stay with me for a few days. You know, Ruth left almost four weeks ago, so there is the second bed available. Are you interested?"

"Of course!" Hilde said. "That's a great idea."

We walked back together. I introduced Hilde to Mrs. Schmitt, and to my surprise she immediately agreed that Hilde could move in with me for the remainder of the month of April. Presumably, the rent for the apartment was paid up by the military until the end of the month, and I made it clear to my landlady that we—Hilde and I—would leave on May 1 at the latest.

That particular day always had been a big holiday for the German government, called *Tag der Arbeit*, Labor Day. In the past years, it had never rained on May 1, and even the radio's weatherman commonly called it *"Führer Weather."* In the past years, numerous May Day parades had been orchestrated with their usual military flair and pomp, including large marching bands strutting their stuff in pure sunshine.

I counted on it: the first day of May would be sunny and warm this year as well. In my mind, the 320-mile march home sounded difficult enough even in good weather, but most likely would be absolute misery in the rain.

The meeting at sick bay the very next morning was attended by a good number of girls from the battalion, all still in uniform and most of them visibly upset. Many had already looked for a temporary place to stay with the local farmers. Some of them had been lucky enough to get a small room; others settled for a place in a shed or even in the barn. Everyone felt happy just to find a roof over their heads until they could head for home.

The consensus was to walk home as soon as possible, to get as far west as we could, not knowing if and when the Russian forces would arrive in this part of the country. The start of our return trip, however, was contingent on the arrival of the American troops, because nobody knew what to expect of an occupational force, or what restrictions or boundaries the military may outline for the German population.

In the meantime, we intended to hurry to Hilde's battery and get her possessions. I suggested we borrow a small wagon from the landlady plus a shovel and an old blanket.

"What on earth do you want a wagon for?" Hilde wondered.

"Do you remember where the surplus gasoline canisters were buried within your battery grounds?"

"Of course I do—I helped dig the holes. What do you want with the gasoline?"

"Well, I was thinking. I've heard there are still motorcycles parked at the quartermaster shed. I know how to ride a motorcycle. I used to ride a 250cc DKW (*Deutsche Kraftwerke*) when I was eighteen years old. If we could get ahold of a cycle, we could ride home in style, provided we had gasoline. So, I say let's get the gasoline today, and maybe we can steal a motorcycle tomorrow.

"According to another rumor," I continued, "quite a few members from the battalion helped themselves to items from the quartermaster. The man in charge allegedly left the day before, and our leaders from the labor service are also gone. As of now, we are strictly on our own. We should get blankets and bedsheets, if possible. We need items we can barter with along the way. Let's get over there afterward and see what we can find, all right?"

Off we went with the landlady's wagon. The battery was deserted. Hilde showed me the location of the buried gasoline, and I retrieved one canister with my little shovel. I loaded it into the wagon and covered it with the old blanket while Hilde picked up her personal things from her locker and packed them alongside the canister. We rushed back because of a possible encounter with the first American troops and the threat of becoming POWs, as we were still in uniform. We had absolutely no way of knowing just how close the first American troops were. With a running start, we headed to our apartment.

Quite a few civilians passed us on the road. Farmers with handcarts or horse-drawn wagons brought in the last beets and potatoes, customarily stored in their fields. Specially prepared *Mieten*, wood-and-rock chambers several feet underground with mounds of dirt heaped on top, kept vegetables from freezing.

From a distance, I spotted several German soldiers walking in small groups. *I wonder what they will do now?*

Suddenly I heard the sound of an enemy plane coming from a westerly direction. A single plane with its motor roaring and guns blasting flew very low over the road, strafing everything in sight.

"Hit the ditch! Get away from the gasoline canister!" I yelled at Hilde, while I jumped into the nearest ditch, covering my head with both arms. She did the same.

In seconds the street was deserted, as if swept clean with a huge broom. As before, it left me shaken until the plane disappeared in the distance.

With the danger past, I grabbed the shaft of the cart and got it rolling with a hard pull. We took off in a bigger hurry than before, not even hanging around to find out if anybody had been hurt. We heard heavy artillery fire slowly getting louder and louder.

We have to store the gasoline somewhere safe and get ourselves to the shelter in the basement of the Schmitt Factory as fast as possible.

We made it back safely, although out of breath and sweaty, only to be immediately confronted by my former boss, Sergeant Major Werner. He was still in uniform and evidently had been waiting for us. I was absolutely dumbfounded. I had heard through the grapevine that *all* of the staff had left.

"I have the motorcycle, but you have the gasoline," he said, his voice stern and authoritative. "Of course, I have no intention to give you the cycle. So: you better give me the canister."

I was furious, but powerless. Who had informed him about our plan—maybe the landlady again?

My status as a low-ranking *Arbeitsmaid* enabled him to walk away with my booty.

"You dirty SOB," I muttered angrily.

Hilde didn't say a word. She just looked at me, shrugging.

"I hope the American troops will arrive soon," I said. "That'll show him." I grabbed the handle of the wagon and shoved it into the basement.

*   *   *

On April 13, 1945, the first troops arrived. *Lucky 13!* The artillery fire came closer and closer. From the upstairs window of our quarters we observed columns of foreign-looking vehicles approaching over the hill. It was time for us to retreat to the basement.

Everyone from the Schmitt family huddled in the shelter, including their workers and a very ill young soldier still in uniform, a friend of Mr. Schmitt's son. He suffered from lead poisoning and should really have been in a hospital. I briefly wondered how anybody could get lead poisoning, but then put it out of my mind. I was more interested in the goings-on outside.

Cautiously I left the basement for a few minutes and crawled around the nearest corner of the house, facing the main road. My mouth dropped open. I couldn't believe what I saw.

The first American troops, heavily armed, dressed in camouflage uniforms with strange-looking helmets and riding in an assortment of equally strange-looking army vehicles, slowly rolled through town.

Some of the more gutsy German residents stood roadside and waved—a premature and dangerous act; many fiercely loyal German troops and faithful party members were still in and around town. One resident farmer hoisted a large, white flag at the entrance to his farm, only to have it ripped down immediately by one of his neighbors, a loyal party member.

Too apprehensive to stay outside, I returned to the shelter to inform the Schmitt family. In my own mind, I kept happily repeating, *They are here. They are here.*

The burden of a pending court-martial had been lifted from my shoulders; however, the uncertainty of the future weighed me down.

Stories soon circulated about female members of searchlight batteries being taken prisoner, mistreated, and even raped by soldiers of the first infiltrating fighting forces. No one really knew how these awful stories started, or whether they were fact or fiction. But I wasn't about to take a chance.

"First of all, we must get rid of our uniforms," I said to Hilde. "And anything else that would give the slightest hint of our military service. I constantly worry about being taken as a prisoner of war at the last minute by the American forces."

"But we don't have any civilian clothes, remember? We were not allowed to keep any in our possession. However, I do have a heavy sweater still with me."

"Well, we need a skirt or two, so we'll have a change of clothes for our trip home. I can sew fairly well. If nothing else, we can make ourselves skirts, provided we find the right material. I still have my blazer, which I kept in my suitcase, contrary to rules and regulations."

We proceeded to rip out the fine, light-gray woolen lining from our military overcoats. We buried the rest of our uniforms in the Schmitts' backyard, together with the mandatory *Soldbuch* (soldier's identification papers). But we kept our white uniform blouses and intended to replace the swastika-imprinted buttons with regular buttons.

Our landlady definitely must have had a change of heart. Either she was feeling guilty or it had to do with the fact that American troops had arrived and virtually were everywhere. She tried to help Hilde and myself in many ways as if making amends. I remained cool but polite and accepted the loan of her old sewing machine in order to make skirts for Hilde and me. We also thanked her for a handful of white buttons needed for our army blouses.

Eagerly we started on our project. I fashioned the gray material into skirts, and now we each had a skirt and a white blouse. I tried it on together with my old navy-blue blazer. Hilde tried her skirt combined with her heavy sweater. We looked at each other and busted out laughing.

"Hey, don't we look chic?" I asked, and we snickered in unison.

We wore civilian clothes for the first time to our next meeting at sick bay and felt marvelous. Many girls were present, and I urged everyone to do as Hilde and I had done.

"To prevent any problems with the American military, get rid of all army paraphernalia, including army identification of any kind," I said.

My advice prompted consternation. For many years prior to the war, it had been mandatory to always carry a *Kennkarte*, a personal ID card, and doing so had become second nature to everyone.

"How are we going to identify ourselves without any ID at all?" someone asked.

"Well, certainly not with an army ID, unless you want to get arrested as a partisan—you know, a soldier in civilian clothes. That could turn ugly."

"What do you suggest?"

"Do as Hilde and I will do first thing tomorrow morning: go to the local city hall and request a written statement, a pass of sorts, on the town mayor's stationery, bearing your name and home address and with the mayor's signature and official seal. An English translation would be helpful, since we'll have to pass through American checkpoints on our way home. Furthermore, I will request a postscript showing we had been on temporary duty in one of the neighboring towns, in a place of business—a factory or hospital or something similar. It will be an outright lie, but do you think the mayor or his staff care at this point?"

Several girls agreed with my idea and wanted to follow along those lines. Other items of common interest were discussed, but the consensus was to leave for home as soon as possible. All of the girls would head west, with the exception of Hanna, who planned to go east to reach the home of an aunt in a small town somewhere near Dresden.

"Hanna," I said, "I don't think it's a good idea to go straight east, because somewhere along that route, you'll have to pass through Russian lines."

"It's not far to get from here to that suburb of Dresden," Hanna insisted. "I will stay with my aunt until it's safe to return to my home in the west."

"Hilde and I need to get going. We want to stop at the quartermaster's supply room in the basement. We heard that all the staff had left already; maybe there's something left that could be of use to us. So long." We waved and left.

Rummaging around the quartermaster's basement, we found leftover canned goods, a few blankets, white bedsheets and *Flug-Sichttücher*—long, narrow sheets of bright orange material that served as landing markers for airplanes. We grabbed what we could carry and headed back to our quarters with our loot.

"Hilde, this orange cloth has me intrigued. It would make pretty nice-looking skirts for you and me. So far we have only one skirt each, and we should have at least one extra change of clothes for the long journey. Don't you agree?"

"Sure, if you want to go to all that trouble."

"I may as well be doing something while we sit and wait. Besides, I love to sew. It's a far cry from the disciplined activity of the past eight months. It soothes my frayed nerves.

"We shouldn't leave until the end of the month," I continued. "By then we should have a clearer picture of what's going on around the countryside."

We started working with the material. While Hilde cut strips on the bias from one of the white sheets, I cut enough material from the orange fabric to make two A-line skirts finished with white piping. Not satisfied with the look, I made a pattern from heavy paper for a five-inch heart. We cut hearts from the white sheet and pinned them about two inches above the hem, and I sewed them on by machine.

"Gosh, you fabricated a kind of a Bavarian *Dirndl* skirt," Hilde said with a laugh. "But it's cute. It will go with our white blouses."

I was pretty proud of myself. Now we each had two outfits. Our small place looked like a messy dressmaker's shop. Before going to bed, we cleaned it up. We had more errands to run the next day to prepare for our long walk home.

*   *   *

Army Communiqué

April 16, 1945: The Russian Red Army plunges into the heart of Berlin.

April 17, 1945: Hitler's order decrees, "Berlin will always remain German and Vienna will again become part of Germany."

April 25, 1945: American and Russian troops meet for the first time at Torgau on the Elbe River.
Germany's fate seems to be hopeless. But Hitler will not give up. He demands to defend the country "to the last man."

*   *   *

Mr. Schmitt contacted me early the next morning.

"Have you ever handled a team of ponies hitched to a small buggy?" he asked.

"No, I have not, Mr. Schmitt. Is it difficult to learn? And why do you ask?"

"Well, you have met Bernhard, the young soldier staying with us. He is quite sick and must get to a doctor as soon as possible.

"The nearest hospital is in Keyna, about four or five miles from here," he continued. "To be very frank, although I do have the horses and a buggy, I do not dare to get out on the road with the American troops milling about. However you, a young woman in civilian clothes, shouldn't have any problem taking our young patient to the hospital.

"We have given young Bernhard some of my son's clothes, and he'll be warmly wrapped in a blanket. Please, will you try to take him to the emergency? I will give you a crash course in how to handle the horses. I'm sure you can do it. I would be very grateful to you. Please!"

Although I was a bit fearful, my compassionate nature got the upper hand, and I agreed to give it a try. Besides, I felt a strong desire to help.

"But what will I do if I am stopped by an American patrol, and they see my charge wrapped in a blanket? How will I explain it?"

"Give them my address and tell them the young man is a relative of mine. You may say it is an emergency, and you are headed for the nearest hospital in Keyna. However, I feel you will not be accosted."

Mr. Schmitt walked down with me to a small stable on one side of the factory, which housed two adorable chestnut-colored ponies. As we approached, they snorted a couple of times and pranced from side to side in their stalls. I petted them. It wasn't at all difficult to get acquainted with such lovely, friendly little animals.

"What beautiful ponies, Mr. Schmitt. What are their names?"

"Max and Moritz, named after two mischievous boys from a very funny poem by Wilhelm Busch. I'm sure you have read that poem, right?"

"Oh, yes. In school we read many poems and short stories of his. He has a very funny way of expressing himself. Most of his stories are lighthearted, but to the point."

Unlike their mischievous namesakes Max and Moritz, the ponies seemed gentle and well-behaved. It was a case of love at first sight, and I wanted very much to have my first lesson as a wagoner in the parking lot. Mr. Schmitt very patiently helped me hitch the horses. He climbed onto the front seat of the buggy next to me. Soon I learned the intricate art of guiding a team of horses, handling the reins, calling out commands, and using the emergency brake on the side of the seat.

Max and Moritz were high-spirited and anxious to go. Going down a small hill at a fast clip scared me enough to engage the emergency break very gently.

"Very good," said my instructor. "Remember, if you want the ponies to come to a full stop, pull on the reins and shout 'whoa.' At the same time, you pull gently on the brakes. Tie the reins to a post or fence when you get to the hospital and notify the nurse in emergency about your patient in the buggy. Bernhard can explain the conditions of his illness. They will take care of the rest."

"I think I understand. How soon would you want me to go?"

"Well, it's still early enough for you to be back before dark if you leave immediately. Traffic at present time is not heavy; probably mostly American military vehicles are on the road. Bide your time and stay on the extreme right side, and you'll be safe."

Deep down I still felt uneasy about the American convoys, but I ran upstairs and grabbed my new ID papers from the town mayor, a handkerchief, and my comb. By the time I got back to the courtyard, Mr. Schmitt had placed young Bernhard into the back of the buggy, bundled up under a warm blanket. I climbed onto the driver's seat and turned around to check on my patient.

"Hello, Bernhard," I said. "How are you today?"

"Not so great. Thanks for taking me to the hospital. Believe me, it's very much appreciated."

"I'm glad I can be of help. Don't worry, I will try my darnedest to get you there as fast as possible, though Mr. Schmitt cautioned me to go at a moderate speed. I hope you are fairly comfortable back there. Here we go."

I grabbed the reins and slapped them lightly on the ponies' backs.

"Let's go," I shouted and briefly turned around. "Wish us luck, Mr. Schmitt."

The horses leaned into their harness and pulled up the low hill to the main road at a slow speed. Soon their hooves beat the street surface with a rhythmic clippity-clop. Remembering Mr. Schmitt's advice, I kept to the extreme right of the road and watched for any obstacles along the way. An American convoy passed us from the opposite direction. The ponies started a kind of nervous dancing when a heavy truck passed somewhat too close. I took a deep breath and held the reins tightly. Instinctively my left hand grabbed the brake without pulling it.

The wolf whistles I heard from members of the convoy as it passed my buggy caused me to sit up straight and proud. I kept my eyes on the road and smiled, hoping the whistles were meant as a compliment. My fear subsided, and I didn't feel intimidated.

This two-horsepower transportation isn't bad at all. It gets me noticed. As long as everyone looks at me, they won't wonder about my cargo.

From a distance, I spotted the red cross on the roof of a large building to my right, along with ambulances and cars in the parking lot and people milling about. Someone directed me to Emergency, and I pulled as close as possible to the entrance. Hitching the ponies to the nearest rail, I told Bernhard not to worry—I would get emergency personnel and a stretcher for him.

An elderly nurse and her orderly came out with me. They helped a very weak and pale Bernhard out of the buggy and onto the stretcher. I thanked the staff.

"Don't lose courage now, Bernhard. You're finally in good hands. I'm sure you will feel better soon. Good luck to you."

I untied the horses from the post, climbed onto the buggy, and turned it around for the road home. A feeling of tremendous relief came over me to know Bernhard was safe in the hospital. Now I just hoped to make it back without any problem.

When I pulled into the parking lot of the factory, Mr. Schmitt greeted me with a sigh of relief. While unhitching the ponies, I gave him a brief account of what happened. He nodded a couple of times and gave me a big smile.

"Good job, good job," he said and patted me on the shoulder.

"Max and Moritz did a terrific job. They deserve at least a few carrots. May I feed them?"

He gave me apples instead, and I held one on my flat open hand. Max gave a couple of happy snorts before he gobbled the apple. Moritz pranced around, trying to push Max aside to get his share. Finally, with one apple on each outstretched hand, I kept them both happy. The ponies had been wiped down and afterward seemed perfectly happy to be back in their stable. I gave each of them a hug and a pat on the rump.

What beautiful, friendly little ponies. And I'm a bit proud of myself for having had the guts to do what had to be done.

Going back to my quarters, I met the landlady on the staircase.

"Oh, you are back," she said. "How did Bernhard make the trip?"

"Fine. The trip did not seem to bother him too much. However, I noticed he was very tired and seemed relieved when we finally reached the hospital. So was I. Now he'll receive the care he absolutely needs."

Her demeanor toward me was friendlier than before.

"Thanks for your help," she said, "and if I ever can be of help to you or Hilde, please let me know."

"Thanks," I said and walked toward our small place on the second floor, where Hilde puttered around with all kind of odd jobs.

Our thoughts were primarily directed toward reaching our home in the west. Without public transportation, trains, or buses, we knew full well we must walk each of the many miles. We discussed the scary prospect, including the fact that most likely, we'd be forced to walk in a zigzag pattern through a war-torn countryside, since we had only sketchy information concerning which areas to avoid. We knew for a fact to avoid the famous Autobahn crowded with American military vehicles. Some Germans even started joking that it had been built specifically for the American occupational forces.

"How are we going to carry our few belongings?" Hilde asked. "We can't possibly lug them along on our shoulders."

"Well, I have been thinking about that, too. We know Mrs. Schmitt won't let us take her good wagon. A few days ago, I spotted a chassis of a very old baby buggy down in the basement. It's dilapidated but has four good wheels. Maybe if a wooden platform could be fastened to the top, we'd have a dandy little cart. It would hold all of our stuff. Let me talk to Mrs. Schmitt. A short time ago, she offered to help in any way possible."

The very next morning, I contacted Mrs. Schmitt concerning the buggy chassis, and without hesitation she handed it to me. Old Man Schmitt built a rather large, flat wooden box and fastened it to the metal base. He even tied a heavy rope to the front bar with a loop at the end for a handle.

I practiced in the parking lot and learned quickly to pull the cart up a hill, but to let it roll ahead of me downhill while holding on tightly to the rope. It worked great.

"Hilde, let's take a break from packing. I would like to go to sick bay and touch base with the girls who might still be there. All right?"

"Give me a minute to pull myself together. I must look a fright."

After freshening up a bit, we headed to the battalion sick bay and met with a large group of our (former) comrades.

The main subjects were the plans, hopes, and wishes for every girl's return home. Most often expressed was the fear of such a long walk home over many days and many miles.

"Get a map; even a partial map will do," I said. "At least you will know approximately in which direction to go. Wherever and whenever you stop, rely on the advice of the townspeople to guide you. They should know what is going on in their neighborhood and which roads to take or to avoid, right?"

"Makes sense," Anneliese said.

The discussion covered most everything, from clothes to food to money. What scared the more timid souls among us was the safety factor of small groups of women walking in a strange part of the country without much protection.

"Where are we going to find a safe place to sleep at night?" one girl asked.

"What about food?" asked another.

"Who can we ask for help?"

"We don't have much money. How could we pay for anything?"

"What about washing up? Or washing clothes?"

"Hold it," I said. "There are more questions than answers. Play it by ear. Do the best you can. Make use of what little you may have, and help each other. Most of all, don't give up, but hang tough. These are terrible times for everybody."

A commotion at the main door interrupted the meeting. Margot rushed in.

"Hey, girls, please come here," she called. "Help me with an English translation."

Anneliese and I rushed out and were confronted by two black American soldiers pointing to the Coca-Cola sign at the front entrance, to the left of the main door of the former restaurant.

"Sorry, no Coca-Cola," I said in my limited English. "Is not a restaurant. Restaurant kaputt. You like water, maybe?"

They declined the offer of water.

"Thank you," they answered with a big smile on their faces and walked away.

Much later I understood why they declined the offer of water. It was not safe for Americans to drink German water until it had been boiled or a certain tablet had been added to kill harmful bacteria. The occupational military government chlorinated the water overall, much to the regret of Germans, who often complained about awful-tasting drinking water, which made lousy-tasting coffee and worse-tasting tea.

Earlier in the day, Hilde and I had encountered the same two black American soldiers on our way to sick bay. We had never seen a black person before and avoided a confrontation by hurriedly ducking into the nearest hallway of a house. Too many bad rumors circulated about the behavior of American soldiers toward German girls.

Until now, under the National Socialist regime, no different races had lived or were permitted to live in Germany

Our own action on the street had nothing to do with feelings of superiority as espoused by the German regime. Only once, as a very young girl, had I seen a "mulatto man," as he was called then—the offspring of a white girl and an Algerian soldier, a member of the French forces during the Rhine occupation of WWI (1919).

*   *   *

Army Communiqué

April 28, 1945: Benito Mussolini, Germany's ally and "the father of Italian fascism," was shot in Milan by partisan Italians, along with his mistress and eleven others. They were subsequently hung by their heels in a public square of Milan.

April 30, 1945: The maniacal force behind the European war is dead. Adolf Hitler, desperate and bitter over the demise of his beloved German Reich, committed suicide with his mistress, Eva Braun, this date in Berlin. (However, the official German statement reads, "Our Führer died a heroic death in action at the end of his fierce battle . . .")

May 1, 1945: Reichs Propaganda Minister Joseph Goebbels and wife committed suicide after first poisoning their five children.

May 2, 1945: Grand Admiral Karl Dönitz has been named as successor of the Führer.

May 2, 1945: 1,000,000 Axis forces (Germany, Italy, and Japan) surrendered in Italy and Austria.

May 2, 1945: Berlin fell to the Red Army. Approximately 70,000 German soldiers gave up and were taken prisoner.

*   *   *

12

THE LONG ROAD HOME

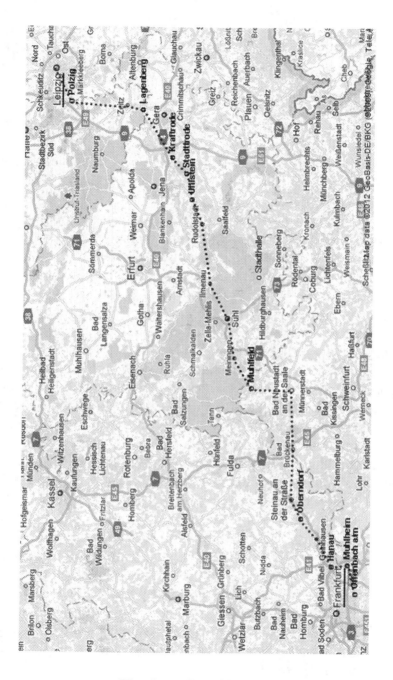

The Long Road Home

The first of May approached, and we briefly discussed the first segment of our route with Old Man Schmitt. He gave us several good pointers. I took notes and put them into my blazer pocket.

Afterward, Hilde and I packed our few clothes and treasures, and then we loaded several quartermaster blankets, bedsheets, and a small amount of food on our little cart. For safety, I carried our food-ration tickets in the pocket of my jacket. We made sure not to forget anything, and all loose ends seemed tied up.

With trepidation and a slight case of nerves, we started very early next morning. Our sheer strong will to get home motivated us. We didn't care one way or another how we would manage; we just needed to try. I had obtained a partial map and knew we must always travel southwest. Our first destination was the town of Gera, approximately twenty-three miles from our starting point of Pölzig. The sun was already up, and the weather promised to be nice.

The Schmitt family wished us well when they bade us good-bye. With a last look and a wave of the hand toward the house, we turned and started walking up the small hill toward the main road.

After several hours, we reached a small, picturesque village along the Elster River. Our march, although very tiring, had gone smoothly. Still in flat country, we passed through several villages with cobblestone streets and dirt roads, seldom with any sign of destruction from the war. Flower boxes in house windows were planted mostly with bright red geraniums. The roadside was sprinkled with the first harbinger of spring: lily of the valley, as well as crocuses and sweet violets. To my delight, I spotted the first pussy willows popping out on bushes lining the road. Spring itself lent buoyancy to our mood.

Hilde and I broke into the first verse of an old spring song: "*Alle Vögel sind schon da ...*" ("All the birds have arrived ...") as we walked on bravely.

We met many travelers, sometimes as many as twenty to fifty, with handcarts, bicycles, and small wagons packed with their belongings. Such wagons were pulled by men or, on rare occasion, by old, skinny horses. We saw a few younger men still dressed in their somewhat disheveled uniforms, like remnants of a lost war. All indications pointed to the war's end, but we were still experiencing it, stuck in the middle at this very time.

We seemed to be participating in a mass exodus, a *Völkerwanderung* on a small scale, reminiscent of the year AD 395, when entire nations moved their tribes from here to there for whatever reason. *How well I remember history class in school.*

"I think for safety reasons we should stay either in front or behind one of these large groups," I said. "If there are only two of us, we might have a better chance of finding lodging at night at one of the farms in the neighborhood."

"I agree."

"Oh, I wish we had a watch. Look, Hilde, the clock on that church steeple says it's close to noon. I think it's time to take a short rest."

"I'm ready for a break, and I am a bit hungry. I also could do with a drink of water. Let's find a water trough. Every village has a trough for their cattle, right?"

We found the trough in the village square with a water fountain and a plain wooden bench next to it. It felt good to sit for a while. *What a wonderful place. Perfect for our first picnic.*

We dug into our food supply, made sandwiches, and jokingly toasted each other with a cup of cold water.

An elderly farmer stopped. He looked puzzled to see two strange city girls all by themselves, having lunch. We gave him a brief explanation.

"Don't walk south to Gera," he said. "It would mean a detour of several miles. Instead cross over the bridge of the Elster River and walk along the secondary road toward Stadtrode. It's a good road with much less traffic. The American troops are everywhere—especially on the main roads and, of course, the Autobahn."

We thanked him for the information, and he wished us luck.

"*Auf Wiedersehen,*" we said.

Crossing the bridge over the river, we found the road the farmer mentioned and kept on walking until early evening. We reached another small, pretty village and decided to stop. Weary from our travels, we thought it was time to look for overnight accommodations (to use the word loosely): a place to sleep in relative safety, with a roof over our heads. Maybe a spare room, a shed, or even a hayloft in a barn—we could not afford to be choosy.

"The sun is setting, Hilde. It must be around 7:00 p.m. Let's take a look at the farms along the road."

"It's a good thing the big group of people ahead walked on without stopping. Our chances of finding a charitable farmer are better."

"Let me go and ask at that farm on the left of the road," I suggested. "Judging by the manure pile on the side of the barn, they must have quite a few animals. Maybe we could even get a free meal. What do you think?"

"No harm in asking. If they turn us down, there's another place farther up. Can't see the manure pile yet, if that's a way to judge a productive farm."

"I was only kidding."

Three steps led to the front door of the modest farmhouse with a large barn on the opposite side. A barking watchdog tied to the corner of the house announced our arrival. A flock of chickens busily scraped and clucked around the manure, and a couple of goats were engaged in a sparring match in the middle of the yard.

I knocked on the heavy, dark, wooden door. An elderly, gray-haired woman wearing a colored cotton dress opened the door. She had a rather pleasant face, with glasses halfway down her nose and a big apron covering her dress.

"Good evening, ma'am," I said. "Pardon my intrusion, but my friend and I are walking home to Frankfurt. This is our first day out, and we wondered if we could possibly stay overnight at your place. We assure you we won't cause you any trouble. We just need a roof over our heads. Please?"

The lady looked us over, turned her head back into the house, and called to someone. An elderly man with a weather-beaten face came to the door. After saying "*Guten Abend*," he nodded and invited us in. *He must be the husband and boss.*

They were curious about where we were coming from and where we were going, so we told our little story, and they sympathized with our lot. Earlier in the day, the old man had talked to other wanderers passing through the village, and all had similar stories, everyone heading for their original homes. He said they all had the same prevalent thoughts of relief that the war seemingly was coming to an end. The farmer had high hopes that his son, too, might finally return home safely from the Russian front.

"My grandchildren need their father," he said, "and I need my son to carry on the farm. I'm getting too old for this backbreaking job."

As the family prepared to sit down for supper in their spacious country kitchen, they invited us to join them, and we jumped at the chance. We hadn't eaten since our picnic at noon. The fresh farmer's bread, homemade sausage, and cheese, all served with big glasses of fresh milk, tasted absolutely wonderful. The old man helped himself to a bottle of beer.

After supper, the farmer's daughter-in-law and the two of us cleared off the table and helped with the dishes. The old lady showed us to the *Kammer*, a windowless, small storage room at the end of the hall, where two cots sat against one wall.

"They are for our grandchildren's occasional visit," the lady said.

We brought in our own sheets and blankets from the cart and placed them on the cots, which pleased the lady of the house. She set a large pitcher of water from the kitchen into a good-sized ceramic washbowl on a small table and then showed us the bathroom, which was situated next to our room. Everything was very plain, but orderly. No shower, no bathtub.

*   *   *

A bathtub in those days was a luxury for most people. The farm reminded me of my life as a teenager at home: we lived in an apartment house on the third floor and didn't have a bathtub, either. I had to break out the large, heavy zinc tub stored in the attic, since there was no room in the apartment itself. In the meantime, my mother put two kettles of water on the gas burner, because the apartment had no hot water heater, either. That, too, was a luxury in those years.

With the towel, sponge, and soap at the ready, I waited impatiently for everyone to go to bed. I bathed in the kitchen, the only warm place in the apartment. When finished, I made sure to empty the tub bucket by bucket into the toilet. It was quite a job, a laborious and troublesome affair. *No wonder we didn't take but one bath per week!*

*   *   *

"Hilde, tell me, did you have a bathtub in your apartment at home?"

"No. Furthermore, our toilet is a half a flight down the main staircase. It's terribly inconvenient."

It was getting late, and we were exhausted. We bade everyone good-night, thanked the farmer and his wife for their hospitality, and headed straight for the bathroom and then to the *Kammer*. Our plan was to get up at the first call of the rooster, just as farmers do.

"Are you comfy, Hilde?" was the last thing I said before I went out like a light. I didn't even remember what or if she answered.

The following morning, as the sun rose on the horizon, we awoke to the sound of animals. The rooster crowed "kickericki" (German roosters don't say "cockle-doodle-do"), the cows mooed, and the pigs squealed. It took us a few seconds to realize our surroundings. We heard the family moving about and knew it was time for us to get up. Waiting for a chance to use the bathroom, we finally made it after the third try. Washing up with the cold water from the pitcher was most invigorating and reminded us of our life in camp. Afterward we poured the dirty water out the back door and into the grass as instructed.

As soon as we finished dressing, the young farm woman came to fetch us for a breakfast of fresh bread, butter, jam, and warm milk. We told our hosts how grateful we felt for their hospitality, then offered a hurried good-bye after retrieving our cart from the hallway.

I grabbed the cart's rope, and off we went to face another day of walking. The nearest crossroad was only a few miles southwest.

We planned the next destination to be Rothenstein, on the Saale River. According to our map, it was located straight south of Jena, a fairly large town. Information passed on to us by local residents urged us to avoid the town of Jena at all costs. Allied troops had already liberated the infamous Buchenwald concentration camp nearby. Nearly fifty thousand prisoners had perished there, but approximately twenty thousand prisoners had been released. Many of those still able to walk were on their way home. Among the liberated prisoners were slave laborers originally from Poland, Hungary, France, Russia, Holland, Belgium, Yugoslavia, Austria, and Italy, along with a few Spaniards who had opposed Franco.

We knew it would be virtually impossible to avoid those numerous and strange wanderers, who harbored nothing but hate and contempt for any German in view of their incarceration and hardship suffered at the hands of German henchmen. To prevent any kind of confrontation, we decided to stay on the opposite side of the Saale River.

Many people gathered at the bridge, the first American checkpoint for us. Sentries with helmets, camouflage uniforms, and MP armbands were posted on either side of the bridge to check everybody's identification papers. I presented our letter from the mayor of Pölzig. The sentry read the English translation, glanced at our cart and us, and then motioned for Hilde and me to move on. He was cool but polite enough, considering he had dealt with quite a mob of foreigners all day long.

Arriving at the town of Rothenstein before noon, we decided to walk through and follow the riverbed on a minor road south. The area seemed virtually untouched by the war: a scenic, almost pastoral landscape of green meadows, lush bushes, and hundreds of fruit trees nestled between rolling hills and blue sky. The Saale River meandered along, the sunbeams reflecting like pure gold in the rushing water. The road started climbing just a bit as we approached the Thüringer Wald, a mountain range of medium height.

*   *   *

Army Communiqué

May 4, 1945: German forces in Holland, North Germany, and Denmark have surrendered.

*   *   *

After another five miles or so (judging from the road signs), we found a beautiful spot off the beaten path by the river where we rested up and had a bite to eat.

"We must eat the remaining luncheon meat, Hilde, before it spoils. And our bread is getting kind of hard, too. Maybe we could buy two days of food supplies in the next village, provided we get there before the stores close."

"How are we doing on money and ration tickets?"

"So far, so good. We didn't spend any money from our last pay as yet, and our ration tickets are good until next week. Help me remember to use them prior to their expiration date. We will be on the road for quite a few more days and must plan accordingly."

This particular spot on the river was very peaceful, and we decided to stretch out in the grass for a longer than normal rest. In a pleasant temperature of about 70 degrees Fahrenheit, we took our jackets off, using them for pillows. As I stretched my legs to get as comfortable as possible, I felt a sharp pain in my right knee.

What on earth? Is this from the long walk? My somewhat tight army shoes? Rheumatism? Naw, it couldn't be, could it? Not at my young age. I've heard old people talk about it, but can young people also be affected by it?

"Hey, I have a sharp pain in my knee. What do you think caused it, Hilde?"

"I don't know. Maybe just overexertion. Give it a rest. Take off your shoes for a while, and elevate your leg."

I did and after a few minutes, the pain subsided. *Nothing to worry about.* I relaxed in the lush grass with the smell of spring all around us. Watching the sparrows in the nearby tree and following small white clouds drifting leisurely in the sky, I almost felt content to just lie here for a while.

But soon my inner drive to get home surfaced again.

"Let's get going," I said. "We still have a long way to go."

Packing up, we headed back to the road leading south. For a while, Hilde pulled our cart to give me a rest.

By early evening, we reached Rudolstadt, still on the Saale River. By then, my leg hurt pretty badly, and I limped with a stiff knee most of the way. We looked for quarters along the main road of this tidy little village, but stopped first at a grocery store on the right of the road to buy a few items. The bakery was next door, and afterward I walked in to buy fresh rolls and a small loaf of bread. The elderly saleslady seemed very friendly, but also curious.

"You are not from this area, are you?" she asked.

"No, ma'am. We are on our way to our home in the state of Hessen and have already walked for two days. My friend and I"—I pointed to Hilde standing outside the door watching our cart—"have quite a distance to cover yet. Right now we are looking for a place to sleep. Would you know where we could spend the night with a roof over our heads?"

"Oh," she said, "wait just one minute. I may be able to help you. My neighbor, Mrs. Sattler, lives in an apartment right next door. She's a good soul and might be willing to help out. I'll send my daughter over to fetch her. It won't take but a few minutes."

She instructed her young daughter to go next door to ask Mrs. Sattler to come and see her. I walked outside to inform Hilde and sat down next to her on a small wall by the bakery, waiting for our prospective hostess.

Mrs. Sattler turned out to be a very pleasant, compassionate soul. After listening to our story, she invited us to her apartment on the second floor, offering us the spare room that had once belonged to her son, who had been killed in action a year ago. Mrs. Sattler had suffered greatly over her loss and felt a need to talk, and Hilde and I were more than willing to listen. We had heard so many similar stories and seen so much misery in the past few months that our lot seemed trivial by comparison.

With our cart safely stored away in the basement of the apartment house, we took a bag of sugar and a small bag of salt from our supplies and handed it to Mrs. Sattler. Even salt was in short supply, and she accepted both as a token of our appreciation.

She noticed my bum knee and told me to follow her, reaching for a large bottle from her medicine cabinet in the bathroom.

"An old house remedy," she explained. "I put it up myself. Just certain herbs in wood alcohol, guaranteed to help the healing process and dull the pain."

She instructed me to take off my wool stockings and rub the liquid on my knee with a sponge.

"Repeat this treatment every few hours," she said.

She also invited us to eat. "Come to the table and have a bowl of vegetable soup and rolls. Unfortunately, I don't have any butter, but I hope you'll like your supper anyway."

Hilde answered for both of us. "Mrs. Sattler, this is more than any stranger could expect. Believe us when we say how much we appreciate your kindness."

Supper absolutely hit the spot. We always appeared to be hungry and didn't need any coaching to eat. Afterward, Hilde helped clean off the dishes, while I was excused and told to elevate my leg. Within minutes, we were sitting around the table, absorbed in conversation. Finally, my eyelids got heavier and heavier. I started having trouble following what was being said, and I nodded off for a second.

"Sorry," I mumbled. "Lack of sleep, you know."

"Ach du lieber Gott!" exclaimed Mrs. Sattler. "Look at the time. I'm sorry I kept you up so late. You must forgive me, but I don't have company very often. Guess I got carried away, huh? It was absolutely wonderful to talk to the two of you." She added, "Just for that, I'll let you sleep in in the morning. Will that be all right?"

As sleepy as I was, I would have agreed to anything.

Following Mrs. Sattler's advice to treat my knee with the medicine indeed gave me some relief, along with several hours of almost pain-free sleep.

The next morning, we cleaned up in a nice, almost modern bathroom. It felt like heaven to take a bath. My knee and my leg were completely stiff, although without the usual severe pain.

"You should have your leg examined before it gets worse," our hostess said to me at the breakfast table. "Let's find out if my doctor will see you on short notice. At least he will tell you how to treat your leg."

"Guess you're right, Mrs. Sattler. Will you go with me?"

"Of course."

The three of us walked into the village after breakfast. The doctor's office was on the ground floor of a two-story building, and several patients were already in the waiting room ahead of us. I knew doctors always saw their patients on a "first come, first served" basis, with few exceptions.

After quite a long wait, the receptionist finally called my name.

"The doctor will see you now." She ushered me into the examination room.

The gray-haired Dr. Meier was quite elderly and on the stocky side. He wore horn-rimmed glasses and an impeccably white coat. Sitting behind his large desk, he motioned for me to sit down on a chair in front of him.

"*Guten Tag.*" I stated my name and gave him a short rundown about my problem leg. After examination, which included pushing and pulling and hitting my knee with a rubber mallet, he said a few Latin words naming the condition.

"Young lady, your knee is infected. Your leg needs therapy and a long rest. I suggest you check into the nearby hospital until your knee has healed and only then resume your walk."

"Thanks, Doc, but no," I said emphatically. "I can't do it. I must get home. I'll have to manage somehow. Maybe you can prescribe a painkiller? That would help. But I have to get back on the road by tomorrow morning."

He shook his head in disapproval over my decision, but gave me a prescription for medication. When asked about the bill for the examination and his advice, he smiled and patted me on the shoulder.

"Don't worry about that. Mrs. Sattler brought you to me, asking for help, and I was glad to do it. But I still think you should not continue your long journey home with your infected knee."

"Thanks, Doctor. I'll think about it. Your help is very much appreciated. *Auf Wiedersehen!*"

Mrs. Sattler and Hilde had the most curious looks on their faces when I met them in the waiting room. I summarized my visit.

"I'm not going to a hospital," I insisted. "I must get home. I just must."

After a short detour through the village and a stop at the pharmacy for my prescription, we returned to Mrs. Sattler's apartment. She insisted I sit in her easy chair with my leg elevated.

"Take your first medication now." She handed me a glass of water.

"Everybody is bossing me around," I replied with a chuckle, but I quietly took my medication and sat in her chair, only to get up for lunch in the kitchen. The rest of the afternoon was spent with more conversation in the parlor, a little bit of laughter, and a few tears. Mrs. Sattler deeply grieved over the loss of her son, and Hilde and I were bogged down with uncertainty about our families back home. Worse, we had only one chance of getting back: walking many more days through a war-torn, topsy-turvy country.

"Admittedly, up to now, we've been darn lucky," I said. "We've come through simply beautiful places virtually untouched by the war or bombings, and we've met wonderful, helpful, sympathetic people along the way. Let's hope our luck will hold out, and we'll get safely home."

Early the next morning, drizzle had been forecast by the radio weatherman. *Well, I guess we can't be lucky all the time.*

We ate a small breakfast with *Ersatzkaffee,* which to me didn't taste any better here than it did anyplace else. We thanked our hostess from the bottom of our hearts for her assistance and compassion and waved good-bye as we started out.

Under cloudy skies, we turned the corner to reach the road southwest to Uhlstäd, also situated on the Saale River.

After a couple of hours of walking along the river, a light rain started. For a short while, we found cover on a bench under a huge oak tree and ate our lunch, which consisted of good country bread and a few slices of luncheon meat we had purchased the day before. For "dessert," I sliced a piece of bread and put sugar on top. However, when I bit down on the bread, the sugar either slid off or sometimes ended up in my nostrils while I was taking a deep breath. I sneezed and then chuckled at my not-so-clever idea.

Determined to satisfy my sweet tooth, I tried another angle by letting the rain briefly drizzle on the bread before I topped the bread with sugar. It worked as long as I didn't soak the bread too long.

The sun finally made an appearance, chasing away the gray clouds. We resumed walking and let our clothes dry on our bodies.

Approximately five miles later, we reached Rudolstad; from there we trekked several miles straight west to Bad Blankenburg on the Schwarza River, a minor tributary to the Saale. Resting for a short period along the riverbed, we admired the countryside with its rolling hills and large green meadows sprinkled with wildflowers in all colors of the rainbow.

A small truck stopped along the road behind us. Startled, Hilde and I turned around, and our eyes widened. It wasn't a truck from the American forces, but a German vehicle with a local license plate.

The guy must be crazy. Doesn't he know foreign troops are everywhere? Besides, where did he find gasoline? It's reserved for VIPs only or for the war machines.

A nice-looking, older man, neatly dressed in sporty clothes, greeted us with a big smile.

"Hallo. Where are you headed?" he asked in a congenial manner.

We stood up and stepped a bit closer to the truck.

"We are on our way to Ilmenau—that is, if we can make the distance before it gets too dark."

"Well, ladies, you are in luck. I live in Ilmenau. I'll be glad to give you a lift. It will save you fourteen miles of walking. Incidentally, my name is Becker—Richard Becker."

I hesitated. *He looks all right to me. What a break.*

"Thanks, Mr. Becker. We really appreciate your offer," I said. "This is my friend Hilde, and my name is Ilsa."

"Let me help you put your cart in the back of the truck, and the two of you can sit in the cab with me."

As the cart was loaded, I noticed large, dark bloodstains in the truck bed, although the platform was completely empty. I took a small step backward. All sorts of thoughts raced through my brain. *What the heck caused this residue of blood? A mishap? Accident? . . . Killing?*

Bewildered, I looked from Hilde to the driver and back to the truck. *Did I misjudge him? Mr. Becker made a very good first impression on an old skeptic like me, but—*

He noticed my hesitation and puzzled look.

"Sorry about the bloody mess. I just came back from my silver fox farm a few miles from here. Every day I come out to feed the foxes with fresh meat, the kind not safe for human consumption. You know, meat that has been contaminated and is not approved by the meat inspector. On my way to the farm, I pick it up from the local slaughterhouse. Unfortunately it's always a bit messy."

"Silver foxes?" I said in disbelief. "In this part of the country? I always thought you find those only in Russia or Norway."

"Not at all," he said. "I have raised this type of fox for several years. It is a very interesting hobby that could probably be very profitable if it weren't for the war. Even high society is not interested in silver fox furs at this point in time."

Darn! Now I don't know what to do. It would feel awfully nice to ride in a car and to get off my leg. I'll chance it.

I gave Hilde a little nudge, and we climbed into the cab ahead of Mr. Becker.

"All set?" He smiled and started the truck.

The two of us felt wonderful being driven through a pretty countryside, admiring this and that as we rode along.

"Where exactly are you headed?" he asked.

"Our homes are in Offenbach on the Main River, near Frankfurt," I answered.

"Frankfurt?" he said, astonished. "Gosh, my wife, Marie, is from Frankfurt. Wait until I tell her. You must talk to my wife. She would be interested in your story. She still has relatives there, but has had no contact with anybody as of late. No mail is coming through, and the phone lines are down. Please say you'll talk to my wife."

Hilde and I exchanged a couple of glances, grinned, and agreed to go to his house—at least to meet with his wife.

In the early afternoon, we crossed the Ilm, a small but picturesque little river hugging one side of Ilmenau. We had covered the fourteen miles in less than twenty minutes.

The car came to a final stop at an older, well-kept stucco house at the outskirts of town. With its red-tile roof and beige exterior, it looked absolutely cozy. Numerous window boxes were planted with spring flowers of red and white.

"Come and follow me," Mr. Becker said. "Don't worry about your cart or your belongings. I'll get them later."

He walked to the front door and opened it with his key. We followed him to a small entrance alcove.

"Hallo, Marie, I'm home. Come and see who I brought with me."

His wife, a nice-looking brunette in her early forties dressed in a colorful housedress, appeared from the back of the hallway. Suddenly I got a whiff of lilac. *Must be her perfume.*

With a most astonished expression, she looked us over.

"*Ach Du lieber Gott!*" she exclaimed. "What have we got here?"

"I found these two young ladies along the highway. They looked kind of tired, and I offered them a ride. They are from Frankfurt and on their way home. They've walked all the way from the Leipzig area. Isn't that something?"

Mrs. Becker shook her head in disbelief. "Did my husband tell you that I am originally from Frankfurt?"

Hilde and I nodded.

"I have lived here in Ilmenau for many years, but still have relatives in and around Frankfurt." She interrupted herself quickly and apologized. "Please sit down over there," she said, pointing to the sofa. "You must be tired. Can I get you a cold drink or something?"

"Thank you," Hilde said. "A drink of cold water sounds wonderful."

She disappeared into the kitchen and came back with two glasses of delicious lemonade.

Lemonade? Where did the lemons come from? Oh, yes, from Italy, of course. We probably still trade with Italy and Japan, two of our allies.

Parched with thirst, we gulped down the lemonade in just seconds. The lady of the house and her husband sat opposite us in their easy chairs. They talked briefly to each other in a low voice. Finally, the husband turned to us.

"Well, young ladies, my wife has agreed that you can stay here overnight, if you don't mind sleeping on the living-room couch. We'll get you a couple of pillows and two blankets. What do you think?"

Hilde and I grinned from ear to ear over so much sudden and unexpected hospitality. Deep down inside, we thanked our lucky stars. Again we had met two compassionate souls helping two less fortunate compatriots.

With a big smile, we happily accepted their gracious offer. "*Dankeschön!*" Thank you.

After a generous supper of fresh bread and various luncheon meats served with a delicious cup of tea, Hilde and I helped wash and dry the supper dishes and proceeded to bring in our meager toilet articles to get ready for bed. The blankets and pillows were already on the couch, but another couple of hours passed with interesting and animated conversation before we really turned in. For lack of pajamas, we slept in our underwear, as we had done many times.

A very ornate old grandfather clock stood in one corner of the beautifully furnished living room; the chiming of the hours reminded me of the Big Ben clock tower of London, while a smaller bell regularly announced each quarter of the hour.

But I miserably tossed and turned. Not only did my leg hurt again, but the constant chiming of the clock kept me awake. I found myself counting the seconds with each tick-tock. (It is no small wonder that to this date, I'm not exactly enthused about grandfather clocks, no matter who owns them.)

Early the next morning, Mrs. Becker knocked on the door, opening it slightly.

"Are you awake, girls? The coffee is ready, and the bathroom is available. Go ahead and get cleaned up for breakfast. Mr. Becker has already left for work; he was sorry he couldn't say good-bye personally. He wishes you good luck and a smooth trip home."

Hilde retrieved our clean set of clothes from the cart, and we took turns in the bathroom and happily got dressed.

Within minutes, we were pulling out chairs at the nicely set breakfast table, with its colorful tablecloth and fine china.

"Oh, how beautiful," we both said as we sat down.

Mrs. Becker smiled. "I'm sure breakfast in camp was different, huh?"

We nodded and then munched away on good farmer's bread and home-cooked jam. Even the *Ersatzkaffee* tasted fairly good after the rarity of whole milk was added.

The road beckoned us to resume our long walk. We thanked our gracious hostess and left a big thank-you for Mr. Becker. With a couple of waves as a last farewell, we turned the first corner onto another stretch of a secondary highway.

"What wonderful people," Hilde said.

I added, "We sure were very lucky again, huh?"

The road ahead wound upward on the edge of the Thüringer Wald area. Then it suddenly took a steady climb of approximately 2,700 feet to the town of Suhl, our intended lunch stop. The fair weather had the wonderful smell of spring in the air. A babbling brook curved and turned alongside the dusty road.

We encountered quite a number of wanderers like us. We spotted five girls with backpacks sitting on a grassy knoll by the water. With shoes and socks removed, they dangled their feet in the cold water of the creek. *They must be taking a break from their own long journey.*

We decided to join them. "*Guten Tag. Wie geht's?* You're on your way home, right?"

"That's right," one girl said. "We're going to Kassel. All of us live around that area. Where are you headed?"

"We're following a southwest direction to the town of Offenbach," Hilde answered. "It's near Frankfurt am Main, on the opposite side of the river."

"Take your shoes off and sit a while. This water feels so refreshing; it'll revive your aching feet," said the blonde in the group, who stood almost up to her knees in the water, her pant legs hitched.

"Great idea," I said, and in seconds, Hilde and I were also dangling our feet in the brook.

All along the creek bed, the grass was thick and lush, sprinkled with many wildflowers this early in the season. Robins, sparrows, and even a few swallows circled overhead to catch their lunch on the wing. I took a long and good look around the area, and then I closed my eyes for a few seconds and totally relaxed.

How wonderful to find inner peace, if only for a short while, in pastoral surroundings that can only be found away from big cities. To meet total strangers who all of a sudden seem like old friends, or even soul mates. You can gather new strength and hope from such encounters. We certainly are not alone in our drive to get back to our homes and families.

* * *

Army Communiqué

May 7, 1945: Europe awoke to freedom this morning. Germany has capitulated to Allied demands in a ceremony at 2:41 a.m. All battlefields lie silent.

* * *

A motor vehicle approached, and we all turned our attention to the road. It was one of those totally strange-looking, open vehicles called a jeep. The driver stopped close by, and all four American soldiers got out and walked toward us.

I felt uncomfortable and held my breath. *What do they want?*

They were smiling as they came closer and closer, their hands outstretched.

"The war is over! The war is over!" they kept saying, while trying to shake our hands.

With my limited English, I stumbled over the word "war."

One of the soldiers used his hands and arms, pretending to shoot a rifle, then lowered them toward the ground. "War! ... No more ... It's finished ... Germany surrendered."

I finally grasped the importance of it all and explained it to rest. "*Der Krieg ist zu Ende!* The war is over. Today is the eighth of May, and Germany surrendered."

None of us would ever forget this seemingly small but very important episode in our lives. Four total strangers from the New World, dressed in camouflage uniforms, still carrying rifles and ammunition, extended their hands to us in a gesture of friendship and peace.

It took my breath away, and I kept shaking my head in disbelief. The soldiers motioned us toward their jeep, and one of the guys pulled out a small camera. They wanted to take a picture of us, barefoot and in tattered clothes. All of us smiled and went along with the joke.

"Thank you," they said and handed each of us a small package, which they called "D ration" or something like it.

"*Dankeschön*." Our heads bobbed in appreciation as we repeated our thanks several times.

The soldiers returned to their jeep and drove off in the direction of Suhl.

We were in a tizzy, repeating the words, "The war is over!" We had no radio to listen to, and no one we could ask. What did this all mean?

"Germany really surrendered?"

"Does it mean no more bombings?"

"Does it mean suddenly all guns fell silent?"

"Just think: maybe back home, everyone can sleep through an entire night without having to scramble for the air raid shelter."

"I wonder how much more damage may have been done in my hometown since I left last fall?"

"And I am wondering if all members of my family are still alive and well."

"We all have a million unanswered questions," I said. "We just have to wait and see and hope for the best until the day we may be back with our families."

Our attention turned back to our American presents. Curiosity got the best of us all, and we busily unwrapped the small cardboard boxes. Each contained crackers and cheese, as well as a small can of luncheon meat. Most important was an unusual treat: a bar of chocolate. We had not had any chocolate in months. I looked at the wrapper and tried to decipher the English writing, but with little success, although the word *chocolate* was ever so close to the German word *Schockolade*. I popped the bar into the pocket of my blazer to savor it on the road at a later time.

Hilde and I dried our wet feet and put on socks and shoes to resume our walk. We would go southwest, while the other girls turned in the opposite direction to reach Kassel. We bid them good-bye.

After a very short walk, I reached for the candy in my coat pocket.

"I've got to try this chocolate, Hilde; I just can't curb my craving. Besides, it's getting pretty warm, and I'm afraid the bar might melt in my pocket."

"I think I'll try mine, too."

"Mmm . . . good," we mumbled in unison. Another munch. "Mmm . . . Good."

Marching at a good pace in our desire to reach the town of Meiningen on the Werra River, we pushed on with almost the last of our strength. In the early evening, tired and hungry, we finally reached the outskirts of town. I spotted a modest little house along the main road. An elderly woman outside was busily watering the flowers in the window boxes near the front door. I boldly walked over.

"Good evening, ma'am. Oh, your flowers are really beautiful. You must have a green thumb."

With a smile and curious look, she turned to me. "Where on earth did you two young ladies come from?"

"My friend, Hilde, and I started out from a small town near Leipzig. We have been on the road for several days on our way to our homes near Frankfurt on the Main River."

The woman shook her head in wonder.

"Right now we need a place to spend the night," I continued. "Would you be able to help us? We are dead tired and cannot go on. I assure you we'd be no trouble to anybody.

We don't relish the thought of camping alone out in the field somewhere."

She put her sprinkling can down by the entrance. "Wait here for just a minute," she said, disappearing into the house. When she reappeared in the doorway, she motioned for us to come in.

"You can stay with us for the night," she said. "Store your cart in the entranceway, and come to the living room." She pointed to an open door to her left in the hallway.

Her husband, a chubby man dressed in work clothes, greeted us at the door. He had a weather-beaten, pleasant face and wore dark-rimmed glasses.

"Hello," he said in a friendly voice. He grabbed our cart and stored it into the corner of the hallway. "You can stay overnight," he repeated. "Come on in and sit down. My wife tells me you are going home—somewhere near Frankfurt?"

"Yes, that's right. We were released from our service with a searchlight battery and told to go home, just like that. There is no public transportation, and we are forced to walk every step of the way."

"How on earth can you cope with the difficulties you surely must have encountered?"

"Lucky for us, we have met nice people like you, who are willing to lend a helping hand. Believe me, it is very much appreciated."

"These are terrible times," the man said.

"Just terrible," his wife repeated, shaking her head, before excusing herself to go to the kitchen.

"Anna," he called, "how about some bread and sausages for our guests? I'm sure they are hungry. Bring the apple cider, too. I placed a couple of bottles at the foot of the basement stairs to keep them cool."

Sitting at the kitchen table, we related the abbreviated version of our story. Subsequently, he told us about their lives in Meiningen, a midsize town of approximately twenty-five thousand people situated between rolling hills of the Thüringer

Wald. They were natives and had lived in their present house for many years.

"Did you know," he asked us, "that Meiningen, for many years, long before the war started, boasted about its very pretty *Schauspielhaus*, a theater? It thrived under a talented music director and was the pride and joy of us all. Now it's in ruins, hit by an Allied bomb. I'm sure in due time it will be rebuilt, provided the money can be raised for such a venture.

"However," he continued, "our prison down the road withstood the war—although the guards at present time are mainly former prisoners, and now the inmates are their former guards and tormentors.

"Which reminds me: if you are leaving tomorrow in that direction, give the prison building a wide berth."

Old Man Müller, a former railroad official, knew many stories about his town. We learned about a special plant that existed for the sole purpose of restoring old steam engines—this especially fascinated me since, prior to my induction, I had worked for the Autobahn Oberste Bauleitung, which at that time was still part of the Federal Railroad headquarters in Frankfurt am Main.

Our conversation slowed down when Mrs. Müller entered, carrying a tray of food and beverages. Hilde and I helped to set the table, both of us smacking our lips in anticipation. The aroma of country sausage, farmer's bread, and cool cider enticed our palates.

After supper we all settled in the living room. Soon I started yawning and found it necessary to apologize.

"We better let the girls turn in, Karl. I'll check the spare room to make sure everything is in order."

Mrs. Müller turned to us. "Go get ready for bed. The bathroom down the hall is not occupied, and your room will be ready in just a minute. I do hope you sleep well."

Hilde retrieved a few items from our cart and disappeared into the bathroom. We bid our host family good-night.

During the night, my leg started to act up again, but in spite of it, I drifted off in a somewhat restless sleep.

We awoke to a beautiful, sunny, and warm morning and heard Mrs. Müller already busy in the kitchen.

"Time to get up, Hilde," I said. But before dressing myself, I gave my leg a good rubdown with the ointment. When Hilde was finished in the bathroom, it was my turn for a quick cleanup job.

We said "Good morning" as we entered the breakfast area, set up in one corner of the sunny kitchen. The smell of coffee drifted under my nose.

After a leisurely breakfast and light talk, our inner drive got the upper hand, and we bade our host family good-bye. Facing at least four more days of walking, we anxiously hit the road. We headed toward the town of Neustadt on the Saale River, avoiding the area around the prison by a couple of miles.

We found quarters for one night with sympathetic townspeople in Neustadt. The very next night, after another long day of walking, we lodged for the night in Brückenau on the Sinn River. Another full day of wandering led us through and over the Spessart Mountain until we finally reached familiar territory in Gelnhausen on the Kinzig.

Although excited about closing in on our destination, we were confronted with much more destruction in and around this larger town. Many of its various industries and important factories evidently had made it an enemy target. But numerous apartment houses and singular dwellings in residential areas were also indiscriminately smashed to smithereens. Entire areas had suffered the death of many unsuspecting civilians and the loss of property.

Throughout the next two days, we faced the same rubble, bomb-site craters, and destruction. Of many buildings and houses, only hollow, blackened facades remained. The closer we moved toward our hometown of Offenbach, a large industrial town of approximately one hundred thousand with important tool and machine factories, the heavier our hearts felt. The destruction there would be at least as bad, if not worse. What had been the fate of our loved ones?

Wherever we went, the so-called *Trümmer-Frauen* (rubble women) worked hard in unison, shoulder to shoulder, clearing debris from houses and surrounding streets. With shovels, brooms, rakes, and every other imaginable tool, they made enough headway that some of them could occupy a small space in the basement of their former dwellings, or even in a shed on a piece of property that formerly had been their garden. It seemed extraordinary how neighbors or total strangers helped each other in a time of such a unique and absolute emergency.

Trümmer-Frauen
Female workers clearing rubble

On the outskirts of town, we spotted a shady place under a tree where we sat down for a rest.

"I was just thinking, Hilde." I leaned my head against the trunk of a tree while talking. "We ought to stop at my weekend cabin on the Grüne See. It's still a day's walk, but it's on the way. I left the key for the cabin with a friend at a small farm nearby. I have bathing suits and clean towels at the cabin. We could take a wonderful swim before we start on the last leg of our journey to see our families. Our clothes are dirty and messy, but at least we'd be clean underneath."

"Great idea, since we haven't had a bath in more than a week," she said with a laugh. "But tell me: how did you get this summer cabin? You never mentioned it before."

"Well, with all the other problems I've had in the past couple of weeks, I really never gave it much of a thought until now.

"It's just a one-room cabin, a former construction shack from the Autobahn Oberste Bauleitung, Frankfurt, where I used to work. Several years ago, many of the older or partially damaged shacks were sold for very reasonable prices. My boyfriend, Jake, urged me to check into it, and I was able to acquire one not too dilapidated for a good price. Since I was well acquainted with the man in charge of sales, I even managed to have the shack delivered in pieces to its present site. Jake and his friends put it together, and then I got busy with the interior decorations.

"It always has been a wonderful place to spend the summer weekends, with all the conveniences of home, so to speak. Wait until you see it—"

I struggled to my feet. "That settles it. Move it. I can already feel that refreshing water."

The next day, we reached the town of Hanau on the Main River. It had also sustained heavy damage by air raids and looked ravaged and desolate. Here, too, the *Trümmer-Frauen* were hard at work. Seldom, if ever, did we see any men, with the exception of the very young or the very old. Most eligible men had been called into military service and would probably return home much later, unless they had been killed in this hell of a war.

Within the crew of the *Trümmer-Frauen,* one could recognize the proverbial stubbornness of the average German, combined with a good amount of diligence and hard work.

We walked on, and at the first glimpse of the Main River, which also eventually runs along our hometown of Offenbach, we gave a joyful shout. It was like greeting an old friend. The hawthorn trees along both sides of the riverbank were in full bloom. Clusters of red and white blooms painted a colorful picture against the blue sky, which was reflected in the shimmering water of the river. With adrenaline flowing from this boost to our morale, we crossed the old iron bridge to reach a small village on the other side of town.

A group of five people, two women and three men, walked with enthusiasm in our direction and greeted us in Russian. *Do they think we are Russians? We must look as tired and disheveled as they do.*

Quickly I tried to remember the few words of Russian my brother Otto had taught me.

"*Ne Rooski*," I said with a smile. "*Ya nee paneemayoo.* (Not Russian. I do not understand.)"

We passed each other on the bridge, and they said, "*Da sveedanneeya.*"

I knew it meant "Good-bye," so I waved.

"Do you think, Hilde, that they were compulsory workers—you know, brought in by the German government from various countries to increase the decimated German workforce?"

"Could be. They walk due east, and that's the general direction of Russia. They probably want to get back home, like us. We can only hope they make it."

After few more miles of walking, we arrived at Dietesheim, a small village located near two minor lakes, Grüne See and Blaue See, so named because one had green water and the other looked very blue.

"Hilda, the cabin is just a little way from here," I said.

Although tired, we picked up the pace and hurried on. As we reached the other side of the wooded area around the lake, I could see the cabin and immediately noticed the open shutters on the cabin. A bicycle was propped up against the shady side of the wall. *What? Who's using my cabin?*

My summer home

We hurried on and finally saw a man sitting on a cot in front of the open door.

"Oh, my gosh, Hilde, it's my brother Hans—Hans!" I called. "Hans!" I felt my eyes tearing up.

Hans sprang to his feet, rushing forward to give me a bear hug. Stepping back, but still holding my hands, he looked at me in total surprise.

"Wow, it's good to see you. Where on earth did you both come from?"

"Leipzig." I wiped a tear from my cheek. "And it took thirteen days, the longest walk of my life. Hans, how is Mama? And Leni and Heidi? Are they all right?"

"Yes, they are. Don't worry. I'll tell you all about it in a minute."

"Hans, do you remember my friend Hilde? She lived with her parents a couple of blocks from Mama."

"I remember her name. I think it's been a while since I last saw Hilde," he said with a chuckle.

They shook hands, and then he motioned for us to step into the cabin.

The inside had remained just as I remembered it, although more than a year had passed since I had seen it last. The comfortable couch sat in one corner, with a small kitchen table and four chairs on the opposite wall. Next to it was a low dresser painted in bright red lacquer and an old-fashioned, cute, black kitchen stove beneath one of the windows.

Ah, my home away from home.

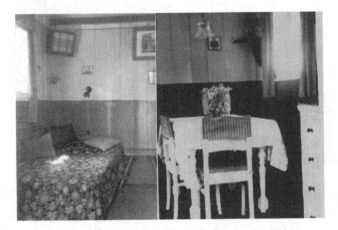

Living room, dining room

Tired but happy, we sat around the kitchen table.

"What are you doing here, Hans?" I asked.

"Well, I walked all the way from the Italian border after escaping from an American truck full of German POW's several days ago. I am hiding in your cabin to avoid recapture by a member of the American forces. With Germany's surrender five days ago, I guess I needn't worry, but there's a great amount of confusion. Nobody knows exactly what to expect or what to do, so I thought I'd stay put until the air clears."

"Please tell me about how things are at home."

"Everybody is as well as can be expected under the circumstances. Our entire family had to vacate their home for a while by order of the US forces. All moved in with Aunt Ria in the next block. After a week or so, they were allowed back into their home. Mama survived a bout with pneumonia but is doing fine now."

He turned to Hilde. "As far as I know, everything is all right on your block, too. Neighbors keep in touch with each other these days. I'm sure my mother would have heard any distressing news by now."

"Will you walk with us to Offenbach, please?" I asked. "Or do you think it is too dangerous for you?"

"I'll just have to take that chance."

"But first, Hans, we both really would like to go for a quick swim. I have bathing suits and towels here in the cabin. Excuse us for a minute while we change."

Soon, Hilde and I plunged into the cool, green water and swam with renewed energy. Standing waist deep, we scrubbed our bodies with vigor, then floated for a minute to relax. *I've never enjoyed such a refreshing swim in my life. I don't think I'll ever forget it.*

Anxious to finally get to our homes, we cut our swim short and went back to the cabin to get dressed. Unfortunately, we had to slip back into our old, dirty clothes. Now I wished I had always kept a set of clean clothes somewhere in the cabin.

Within minutes and with great anticipation, we started on our last stretch to our home in Offenbach. My leg was still hurting, so Hans suggested I sit on the saddle of the bike while he pushed it. Hilde pulled our little cart.

During our lively three-way conversation, we reached our home in Offenbach in a seemingly short time. A quick glance around the old neighborhood revealed quite a bit of destruction, but our house was still standing, although showing a certain amount of damage. My thoughts were full of compassion for our neighbors who had suffered through the many raids, but at the same, time I felt happy about the relatively good condition of our own house.

"I will walk Hilde the rest of the way to her home," Hans said. "Why don't you run upstairs and surprise Mama?"

"Good-bye, Hilde. Give your parents my best regards. I'll see you in a few days, as soon as I have rested up a bit. So long."

Flustered, thrilled, and shaking with excitement, I rushed upstairs. Before I knocked on the door to the apartment, I took a deep breath to calm myself. When Mama opened the door, I threw my arms around her and cried, "Mama, I'm home!"

ABOUT THE AUTHOR

Ilsa Fanchin was born and educated in Germany. Five months after the war ended in 1945, she worked for the American military government as secretary, interpreter, and translator. She met and wed American Sergeant Major Fanchin—now deceased—and came with him to America at the end of his tour of duty.

She lives in Laguna Woods, California, and has kept in touch with her many German friends. She serves as their personal tour guide when they visit California.